Chris Cosentino
BEGINNINGS
My way to start a meal

Chris Cosentino

BEGINNINGS

My way to start a meal

photographs by Michael Harlan Turkell

OLIVE PRESS

Olive Press

Recipes and text © copyright 2012 by Chris Cosentino

Images © copyright 2012 by Michael Harlan Turkell

Illustrations on pages 158–159, 180–182 © Simone D'Armini

Olive Press is an imprint of Weldon Owen, Inc. and Williams-Sonoma, Inc.

Weldon Owen, Inc. is a division of Bonnier Corporation

415 Jackson Street, Suite 200, San Francisco, CA 94111

Library of Congress Control Number 2011945003

ISBN 978-1-61628-294-3

www.wopublishing.com

www.williams-sonoma.com

Color separations in Hong Kong by Mission Productions

Printed and bound in China by Toppan-Leefung

First printed in 2012

10 9 8 7 6 5 4 3 2

For my wife, Tatiana, and my son, Easton,
thank you for always being the rays of light in my life.

contents

CHRIS WORKED FOR ME AT RUBICON IN 1996. HE WAS WET BEHIND THE EARS.

He had just landed from the East Coast, and talked incessantly. Could he cook? Yes. However, this was back in the day when I ruled my kitchen by fear, discipline, and quiet. We had a blinding amount of talent behind the helm and we were dead serious about everything that we prepared. Chris had a shock of wild, bleach-blond hair, endless energy and curiosity, and a really big mouth. Early on, I branded him with the name "Hollywood," which was often heard in the kitchen with phrases like: "Hollywood, shut the (expletive) up." Of course, this shouting at him had no particular effect. Chris was a good guy, obviously talented and dedicated, and he definitely stood out.

In 2002, I got to know the other half of Chris—his lovely, smart, and super-cool wife, Tatiana. It is a huge compliment to Chris and a testament to his dedication, intelligence, and great taste that he has been married to Tatiana for 11 years. In our business, it takes a miracle and the right partner to find relationship success, and it couldn't be more important to have both of these things on your side as you pursue a culinary career. There are many characteristics, decisions, turns of luck, and moments that make a great chef. And it takes a lot to hold it together for all the years that lead up to owning a restaurant or business, gaining a slot on TV, acquiring a book project, or any other opportunity in our crazy profession. Knowing them both, I recognize that Chris cherishes Tatiana and all that she contributes to his success, as well as the stability that she provides to him. She is his touchstone. I know that Chris appreciates his wife and gorgeous son and he knows how they have contributed to the successful chef that he is today.

I tracked Chris's career a bit after he left my restaurant, though I cannot say we were super-close for the years immediately following our working relationship. I saw from afar how he developed and was impressed with the turns in his career, the decisions he made, and how he took on new endeavors. I mainly saw Chris at the farmers' market and heard what he was up to from numerous mutual associates. He continued to develop an interest in sustainability and sourcing. But after he took over at Incanto, I saw how much Chris had developed as a chef and as a person. I noticed that he had gone whole hog into everything Italian: pasta, salumi, and whole-animal cookery. Clearly he had been on a campaign to learn as much as possible and develop his own style and passion. And he became the Offal King.

Chris and I crashed into each other full force in 2007 while filming the first season of The Next Iron Chef. It was great to see a familiar face in the chaos that was that show. We went through major trauma together and bonded once again, this time deeply. Though I did not last long on the show, Chris was an absolute rock for me—the mentee was supporting the mentor—and it was a beautiful new phase. As Chris flourished on the show, he would call me along the way for support and encouragement and has continued to do so ever since. Chris doesn't really need my advice, as he has great instincts and makes the right choices; I guess he just likes the confirmation that he is doing it all right.

Since then, Chris has gone on to open the amazing salumi company, Boccalone; he has become a TV star; and he has now written this beautiful book. Chris is always the master of the unexpected, and in these pages he exemplifies the complexity that is Chef Cosentino. Everyone probably expected Chris's first book to be all about offal, but here he has shown his gentle way with delicate seasonal produce and a good deal of refined and beautiful food—along with just a hint of the guts and glory that he is known for. The recipes are great, as is his story. The book's format is novel. And the food looks really delicious. I can't wait to give it to my friends and family and look forward to enjoying it as part of my own cookbook collection.

I know that there is much more to come from Chris. He will continue to bring us delicious food at Incanto, Boccalone, and beyond; he will continue to entertain us in the media with his irrepressible nature; and he will, no doubt, inspire us to push our own limits as he continues to do so in his own food, life, and career.

TRACI DES JARDINS, JARDINIERE

I SAT AT A TABLE IN FRONT OF INCANTO'S MAIN DINING ROOM.

I watched Chris pull up outside. With his fixed-gear bicycle, shoulder bag, light-blue "fauxhawk," and tattoos, he had the edgy look of an urban bike messenger.

Incanto was facing its first major fork in the road since opening ten months earlier; a new chef. Chris was the first of two dozen candidates I interviewed for the job. Observing Chris's arrival, I couldn't help but think, "That's Incanto's next chef."

We sat down and talked about food, our childhoods (both in southern New England), and old cookbooks. Though Chris had not yet been to Italy, he was an avid cookbook collector. After our first tastings, I soon realized his abilities in the kitchen surpassed even the best of my culinary experiences during my dozen or so visits to Italy.

That day, April 22, 2003, marked the start of a special friendship. We share love for tradition, belief in doing things the hard way, and a healthy streak of stubborn craziness. Our differences: One is a wizard with a knife, the other with a spreadsheet.

If you're new to Chris Cosentino, this book will introduce some of the things I most admire about him, both as person and chef: His deep respect for nearly-forgotten ways of approaching food. His relentless curiosity, an endless quest for undiscovered ingredients, techniques, and flavors. And lastly, his natural gift for explaining at times complex concepts about food and cooking.

This book is titled "Beginnings" not merely because it's about dishes meant to be served at the start of a meal. Chris has so much to contribute that a single book won't likely be sufficient. I, for one, will be watching with great anticipation to see what comes next.

MARK PASTORE, INCANTO

FROM WHERE I SIT, THERE ARE THREE DISTINCT STYLES OF COOKBOOKS THESE DAYS.

First, there's the cookbook that's written by a TV chef—someone who doesn't have a restaurant, but wants to capitalize on their star power. Then, there's the cookbook that basically treats everybody like they're a novice, touching on every detail of what the dish should look like and how long it will take to make it. Finally, there are the professional cookbooks, which most people don't understand unless they are in the field. I didn't want to write any of these.

I think that the best cookbooks are the old-fashioned ones that I've been collecting forever, such as *The Boston Cooking-School Cookbook* by Fanny Farmer. Those old books are so good because they just tell you what to do and let you take it from there. They might say, "Today we're making Brunswick Stew. Catch a squirrel in your backyard, skin it, gut it, save the tasty bits. Break down the squirrel into quarters. Dust it in flour, season it, and sear it in lard." Those books gave you very distinct techniques, but they didn't baby you or hold your hand through the process. When these books were published, there was an expected understanding of the basics, and you just got on with it and cooked

the food. My hope is that this book is more like those books I love from long ago, and less like those that crowd the marketplace today. I believe that when you challenge people with an unfamiliar technique, or a new flavor, or an interesting ingredient, it makes them think. And when people think, they learn. From my perspective, anytime you cook and you reach a moment when you are uncomfortable, you have to figure it out. Then, you learn something. And it's a good feeling. I hope that you will learn something from these pages.

This book is a collection of Italian-style first courses based on my experiences over time. For example, I grew up in New England, so lobster was a big part of my childhood. That's why I put a great lobster dish in here. When I worked for Mark Miller, he taught me to love quail. Also, when I moved to Northern California, I would see wild quail while mountain-biking in the headlands. So quail has a spot in the book. I base a lot of my food in history, so some of the recipes use an old recipe, but modernize it for today. Each recipe has a story, and I've included these stories throughout the book.

I organized the recipes seasonally because I think everybody in the country, except for in a few select places, eats seasonally. Defining this book by seasons gives you an understanding of what to look for in your markets and what ingredients will help make your food taste best. It's how I cook in my restaurant. Take tomatoes, for example: A tomato in February tastes like cardboard, but a tomato in late summer tastes sweet and refreshing. In those months, my goal is to kill you with tomatoes, so you never want to see another tomato until next August.

Most people know me as a meat lover, but I actually think vegetables are really interesting and they play a major role in this book. Each vegetable has its own terroir, which I love to play up. If you think about it, it's kind of like treating vegetables like you would meat, and showing off their best qualities.

I don't really know if this book will appeal to my professional chef colleagues, or to the home cook, or both. I just want it to represent what I do and who I am without compromising along the way. You may be surprised by some of the things you find in here because it shows a distinctly different side of me than a lot of people expect. Yes, this book is Italian in its subject matter, but we don't live in Italy, so this isn't technically Italian food—it's more of an Italian philosophy of food. I like to say that I live in an area of Italy called California. We have very similar climates, and very similar things are grown, harvested, raised, and manufactured close by: olive oil; great wines; amazing meats; and abundant, locally farmed produce. But food here is never going to taste the same as it does in Italy because we're in a different place. These recipes are not Cal-Med food, or Cal-Ital food; they're just my interpretation of Italian food.

You won't need to buy all sorts of fancy tools to cook my recipes. All you need are the basics: a good knife, a sturdy vegetable peeler, some pots and pans, a grill—you know, cooking shouldn't be too hard. At the end of the day, I put things in this book that I felt were fun. I didn't want this book to be the same old stuff you always see. I didn't want to do fava beans on a piece of grilled bread with pecorino and mint. Everybody's seen it. Everybody's done it. Not that those things are wrong, it's just not what I want to do.

I'm always thinking about food in a new way, but I'm not trying to reinvent the wheel. It's more like I'm stopping and looking again at what's been done and then presenting it my way. My food will not change the world, but I do hope you enjoy the journey.

Chris Cosentino

you say salami,

I say salumi

The Italian word salumi (like charcuterie in French) is an all-encompassing term used for all types of prepared meat products, usually made from pork. People have been curing meat for centuries. Before there was refrigeration, curing was the only way to preserve meat or prevent spoilage. The practice of salting and aging meats is found in all cultures around the world, such as Spain, Italy, England, France, China, and the US South—just to name a few—and each culture has its own distinct flavor profile and salt content.

The key to making good salumi is patience, which is hard for a guy like me. My hyperactive tendencies and need for instant gratification make it a big challenge to pack something into a casing and then wait for three to four months before tasting it to see if I made it right or not. Making salumi has been a lesson in patience, but it comes from an appreciation for science and love of learning the old ways of doing things. When I started at Incanto in 2003, I cured meats for the menu in small batches, but they proved so popular, it got to a point where I couldn't keep up with the demand. It was then that my salumi company, Boccalone, was born.

FRESH SAUSAGE

Making sausage is a logical outcome of efficient butchery; it's a balance of lean meat to fat and spices. The meat and fat are ground, mixed with herbs, spices, and wine, then stuffed into a casing made from the cleaned intestine of the pig or lamb, producing the characteristic torpedo shape. In traditional sausage making, if there were no intestines available, the inner lacy fat, known as caul fat, would be used to create a patty-shaped crepinette.

1. Italian Sausage

This sausage can range from mild to a downright inferno, depending on the producer. The mixture of ground meat, fat, and spices are stuffed into a hog casing. I like it served in a bun with a dollop of aioli or on a pile of peppers and onions, or removed from the casing and sautéed for a pasta of orecchiette and broccoli rabe.

2. Breakfast Sausage

A finely ground traditional English-style breakfast sausage in lamb casings with citrus and sage. We make a version of this at Boccalone that came from the English side of my family who owned Easton's Newport Sausage Company in Rhode Island from 1860 to 1942. Of course, it's not only good for breakfast.

3. Crepinettes (fagetelli)

When casings were unavailable, traditional sausage makers would wrap the sausage patty in caul fat, which resembles lace. Caul fat is the thin fatty membrane lining the intestines of a hog. It is used to help keep the sausage moist and its fat will melt away from the meat as it cooks.

4. Fennel Sausage

This coarse-ground sausage is made from a balance of lean meat, fat, and fennel seed, then stuffed into a hog casing. It is on the sweeter (meaning non-spicy) side of the sausage spectrum. I grew up eating this type of sausage, which is perfect for a traditional New England clam bake.

CURED-TO-COOK SALUMI

These popular types of salumi are made from the belly and jowl of the hog. Each is cured with a unique blend of salt and seasonings, but they still need to be cooked before serving. I recommend having at least one of these around at all times in your refrigerator to add amazing flavor to a variety of dishes.

1. Pancetta

This is skinless pork belly seasoned with spices and rosemary and rolled. You can fry thin slices and eat them as you would breakfast bacon, but I like to wrap it around small birds and roast them. You can also add chopped pancetta to pasta dishes, vegetables—anything, really!

2. Pancetta Affumicata (smoked bacon)

After the curing process, pork bellies are cold-smoked for 4–8 hours to achieve maximum smoky flavor. Along with the salt, the smoke helps to preserve the meat. Different types of wood are used to create different flavors in the meat.

3. Guanciale (face bacon)

The word *guancia* means cheek in Italian. This salt-cured pork jowl originated in central Italy. It is the traditional cured meat used to make the famous pasta dishes carbonara and Amatriciana. Its flavor is both salty and mellow, with a trace of caramel. Use it as you would pancetta.

CURED SALUMI

There are two different categories of cured salumi: those made from intact cuts of whole muscle, such as prosciutto or lonza, and those made from chopped or ground meat, known as salami. In both categories, the curing and fermentation process physically transforms raw meat into something safe and ready to eat. Like making cheese from milk, wine from grapes, or bread from water and flour, the intention is to craft something special, more delicious than the sum of the raw parts.

1. Soppressata

This traditional Calabrian salame packs some serious heat. The meat is coarsely ground and then pressed, which gives it an uneven, rustic appearance when sliced.

2. Nduja

This spreadable, spicy salame originated in Calabria. Its flavor profile—a blend of chiles with hints of bitter orange and warm spice—reflects Southern Italy's African and Moorish heritage. It's perfect on grilled bread, or on pizza or pasta. Or, try it in my creative take on crostini (page 23).

3. Prosciutto

Americans have ham, and Italians have prosciutto, made famous by those of Parma and San Daniele. The best prosciutto is very thinly sliced with a silky, buttery texture and a deep rose color streaked with white fat. Serve it with fresh fruit.

4. Lonza

Similar in both taste and texture to prosciutto, lonza is the back loin that is cured in salt and fennel and air-dried. Slice it thinly and put it in a sandwich, or serve it simply with fresh fruit.

5. Lardo

Also known as prosciutto bianco, this is cured and seasoned pork back fat, but don't let that scare you away. It is creamy, delicate, and flavorful. It is great served on a warm crostino. At Incanto, I serve it with Asian pears (page 141), but it's also good with nectarines or figs.

6. Orange & Wild Fennel Salame

This is a medium-grind salame with a delicate balance of orange zest and wild fennel. Using both wild fennel seed and pollen gives the salame an earthy and distinct fennel flavor.

7. Capocollo

This is made from the eye of the pig shoulder and cured with aromatic spices, which develop and intensify as the meat ages to produce a spicy salame with a strong pork flavor.

8. Ciasculo

I like to call this the northern cousin of *nduja*, but it is soft and creamy, not spreadable. We pack ours with porcini mushrooms to give this salami a huge boost of umami.

9. Salame Pepato

This medium-grind salame is seasoned with three specialty varieties of peppercorns. Each pepper type adds its own character, which combine to create a distinct, but not overpowering peppered salame.

10. Pancetta Piana

This is a dry-cured, skin-on pork belly seasoned with black pepper and rosemary. It is produced in many regions of Italy. It's delicious sliced thinly and served alone, or used to add salty, porky goodness to soups and stews.

11. Brown Sugar & Fennel Salame

A coarsely ground salame, this has an assertive fennel flavor from whole fennel seeds. The brown sugar leaves notes of caramel and molasses that pair beautifully with the fennel.

COOKED SALUMI

Though often considered the poor cousin of dry-cured salumi, cooked salumi offer a variety of flavors, textures, and colors. In addition, their production utilizes a vast array of cooking techniques and styles, including grinding, chopping, brining, pickling, poaching, baking, and braising, to name just a few. Each of these different cooking techniques finds a place in this category.

1. Prosciutto Cotto

This is the Italian version of a city ham. The translation is "cooked ham;" it is often brined with clove, allspice, sugar, and pepper and then slow-cooked. It is delicious eaten in sandwiches.

2. Mortadella

This is the original bologna, a delicate balance of fat, meat, and spice, with pistachios and black peppercorns. Its pillowy texture and smooth flavor make it ideal to eat alone, either sliced thinly or cut into chunks. It also makes great sandwiches.

3. Cotechino

This coarse-ground sausage from Modena is a mixture of lean meat, skin, tough meat cuts, and delicate spices reminiscent of Christmas baked goods. It's traditionally served during the winter holiday season with lentils to symbolize prosperity in the New Year. It can also be sliced thin and served with Salsa Verde (page 162) or with polenta and bitter greens.

4. Sanguinaccio

This traditional northern Italian blood sausage has a light hint of chile and the creaminess of rich pork blood. *Sanguinaccio* is great with eggs or cooked white beans. At Incanto, I serve it in many ways—see My Last Supper on page 180.

5. Ciccioli

Typical of the Emilia-Romagna region, *ciccioli* is prepared by braising scraps of lean meat with fat and skin, and seasoning the mixture with garlic and rosemary. *Ciccioli* has a pleasing, unctuous mouthfeel balanced by the rosemary. It's delicious when eaten alone in thin slices or served on warm bread with pickled onions.

6. Paté di Campagna

This is a traditional Italian paté featuring coarsely ground pork meat, tongue, liver, kidney, blood, herbs, and spices. It's best served at room temperature with whole-grain mustard and grilled bread.

7. Porchetta di Testa

This delicacy is a pig's head that has been treated like the traditional *porchetta* from Tuscany. The meat is seasoned with garlic, rosemary, and chile, and then rolled, tied, and cooked. Slice it for sandwiches or arrange on a plate and sprinkle with capers and shaved Parmigiano-Reggiano.

8. Coppa di Testa

This delicately seasoned salumi, whose name translates to "cup of head," is made from the meat of the pig's head plus the tongue and trotters, all braised until tender and then combined with the cooking juices and spices and allowed to set. Thinly slice it for sandwiches.

6

4

7

5

8

BUILDING A MEAT PLATTER

Setting out a meat platter is my favorite way to start a meal. Here's a primer on how to do it.

choose different types

A great salumi platter relies on having a nice balance of cooked and cured meats to provide different textures and flavors for your guests. As a general guideline, choose a selection of 3 to 5 meats, and at least 1½ ounces (45 g) total per person.

slice meats thinly

If you have a deli-style meat slicer at home, it's best to slice each salume just before serving it so that it doesn't oxidize. Otherwise, ask your local specialty food store or deli to slice the meat thinly and wrap it tightly. Plan to serve the salumi within 2 days of slicing.

arrange items artfully

You don't need to worry about making your meat platter look fancy. Just lay the items on a platter or board in a way that looks nice to you and makes it easy for your guests to access them. Put out small forks or spreaders as desired for serving. Be sure to let the meat come to room temperature before serving so the flavors shine through.

add variety

I like to serve some vegetables with the salumi, which help round out the flavors and cut the richness of the meats. Look for recipes for roasted garlic, pickled onions and carrots, balsamic-roasted cipollini, and more on pages 166–168.

spring

Charred Fava Beans, Mint & Aioli 20

Marinated Sardine & Nduja Crostini 23

Grappa-Cured Arctic Char, Pickled
Red Onion & Watercress 24

Broccoli Rabe & Potato Frittata 27

Barolo Bagna Cauda 29

Sunchokes, Artichokes & Sunflowers 30

Asparagus, Spring Potatoes,
Crème Fraîche & Caviar 32

Artichokes, Mint & Lemon 35

Bean & Radish Salad 36

Pickled Boar, Herb Pesto,
Grilled Onions & Pine Nuts 39

Green Garlic Brodo, Poached Egg
& Fried Bread 41

Egg & Anchovy Crostini 42

Fava Beans, Strawberries & Pecorino 45

Spring Lamb, Anchovy & Mint 46

Fava beans and I have a love-hate relationship. I love it when the first pods of spring arrive in the kitchen, but I hate that it takes hours to shell them. So when some baby ones came in one day, I charred them in the pod and ate them whole. It was a great way to start the fava bean season.

CHARRED FAVA BEANS, MINT & AIOLI

1 lb (500 g) baby fava beans in the pod, pods no more than 3-4 inches (7.5-10 cm) long

2 tbsp olive oil

¼ cup (¼ oz/7 g) fresh mint leaves, torn

Kosher salt and freshly ground black pepper

Aioli (page 161)

Snip the tip and tail of each fava bean pod, making sure to pull off the tough strings that run down the "seams" of the pods.

In a large sauté pan over high heat, warm the olive oil until ripples appear on the surface. Remove the pan from the heat and add the fava beans. Return the pan to high heat and cook the beans, turning as needed to heat evenly, until the pods are charred and golden in spots. Be careful they do not burn. When the pods deflate, they are ready. This should take about 3 minutes. Remove the pan from the heat, add the mint, season with salt, and toss to coat evenly.

Transfer the beans to a warmed platter. Add a large spoonful of the aioli to the platter for dipping, sprinkle the aioli with pepper, and serve right away.

SERVES 4

Remove the strings on both sides of the pods with your fingers

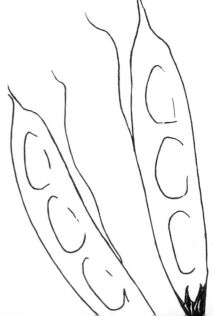

When I went to Spain with my friend chef José Andrés, we ate a dish that combined sardines and sobrassada, a paprika-seasoned cured pork sausage. That pairing inspired this dish. The heat of the nduja, a spicy Calabrian pork salame, helps the flavor of the sardines to "pop"—a perfect balance of land and sea.

MARINATED SARDINE & NDUJA CROSTINI

16 fresh sardine fillets

Kosher salt and freshly ground black pepper

Red pepper flakes for sprinkling

4 tbsp (2 fl oz/60 ml) fresh lemon juice

1 bunch *each* fresh thyme and flat-leaf parsley

5 bay leaves

4 tbsp (2 fl oz/60 ml) dry white wine

Extra-virgin olive oil

3–4 oz (90–125 g) *nduja,* preferably Boccalone brand (see Sources)

2 baby fennel bulbs

1 bunch French breakfast radishes, trimmed

A few small leaves wild arugula

Fresh lemon juice

16 baguette slices, cut on the diagonal ¼ inch (6 mm) thick, and grilled

1 lemon

In a shallow glass or ceramic dish, arrange some of the sardine fillets, skin side down, in a single layer (the number of fillets in each layer will depend on the size of the dish). At this point, estimate the number of sardine layers that you will have. Sprinkle the sardines with salt, pepper flakes, lemon juice, thyme, parsley, bay, and wine so that each layer is sprinkled evenly with the ingredients. Repeat until you have layered all of the sardines and seasonings in the dish. Pour olive oil over the top until the fillets are completely immersed in the oil. Cover and refrigerate for at least 24 hours or up to 3 days.

When ready to serve, remove the sardine fillets from the marinade and discard the marinade. Let the sardines and the *nduja* come to room temperature.

Trim off the stalks from the fennel bulbs and set the fronds aside. Using a mandoline or other vegetable slicer, cut the radishes and fennel bulbs lengthwise paper-thin. Place the radish and fennel slices and arugula in a small bowl, add the fennel fronds, and season to taste with lemon juice, salt, and pepper.

Arrange the bread slices on a tray and rub the top of each slice with the whole lemon, releasing the natural oils of the zest to flavor the bread. Scoop the *nduja* out of its casing and spread a nice even layer on each bread slice. Lay a sardine fillet on top of the sausage, and then arrange a small amount of radish, fennel, and arugula on each sardine. Finish with a drizzle of olive oil and a grind of pepper. Serve right away.

SERVES 4

Curing the char with grappa adds new layers of flavor. I like to pair the char with the bite of both watercress and pickled onions to help balance out the natural richness of the fish. You'll only need one fillet for this recipe, but it's worth curing the whole fish; you can use the second fillet for lox and bagels the next weekend.

GRAPPA-CURED ARCTIC CHAR, PICKLED RED ONION & WATERCRESS

CURED ARCTIC CHAR

5 cups (2½ lb/1.25 kg) kosher salt

2 cups (1 lb/500 g) sugar

12 bay leaves

¼ cup (1 oz/30 g) fennel seeds

2 lemons, quartered

3 cups (4½ oz/140 g) packed fresh fennel fronds

1 whole Arctic char, 3–4 lb (1.5–2 kg), cleaned, filleted with skin intact, and pin bones removed

¼ cup (2 fl oz/60 ml) grappa

¼ cup (1 oz/30 g) Pickled Red Onions (page 167)

1 bunch watercress (about 4 oz/125 g), tough stems removed

(continued)

To cure the arctic char, in a food processor, combine the salt, sugar, bay, fennel seeds, lemons, and fennel fronds and process until the mixture is a green wet mess, about 5 minutes. Using the pointed tip of a knife, poke about a dozen or so shallow holes in the skin side of each char fillet, spacing the holes evenly. This will help the cure penetrate into the flesh of the fish. Rub the fillets on both sides with the grappa, being sure to get it into the holes on the skin side. Layer half of the salt mixture in the bottom of a glass or ceramic baking dish just large enough to hold the fillets. Place the fillets, skin side down, on top of the salt mixture and then top the fillets with the remaining salt mixture. Place a sheet of plastic wrap directly on the surface of the fish, then cover the dish with plastic wrap. Refrigerate for 36 hours.

Rinse the fillets under running cool water and pat dry. Lay the fillets on a platter and place in the refrigerator, uncovered, to air-dry for 24 hours. Turn the fish over and again refrigerate, uncovered, for 24 hours. You will need only one fillet for this recipe. Reserve the second fillet for another use. It can be covered and refrigerated for up to 1 week.

When ready to serve, cut the fish fillet against the grain into 24 paper-thin slices (4 slices per serving). Place the slices between sheets of parchment paper until needed. Put the pickled onions and watercress in a bowl.
(continued)

1 baby fennel bulb
with fronds

Kosher salt and freshly
ground black pepper

1 tbsp extra-virgin olive oil

2 tbsp crème fraîche,
whisked gently

2 tsp finely grated
lemon zest

Trim the stalks and fronds from the fennel bulb. Discard the stalks and reserve 1 tablespoon of the fronds. Using a mandoline or other vegetable slicer, slice the baby fennel bulb lengthwise paper-thin and add to the watercress and onions. Season with salt and pepper. Add the Arctic char slices and the olive oil and toss gently to coat evenly.

To serve, spoon a pool of the crème fraîche on the center of each serving plate and, if desired, use a spoon to spread the crème fraîche in a semi-circular shape around the edge of the plate. Divide the salad evenly among the plates, arranging it on top of the crème fraîche. Top the salads with the lemon zest, reserved fennel fronds, and a grind or two of pepper. Serve right away.

SERVES 6

How to make a proper shmoo
so your plate looks fancy!

①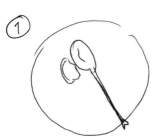

Drop down the creme fraiche

②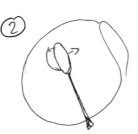

Angle spoon in creme fraiche and drag while turning spoon

③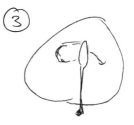

Continue pulling the spoon to spread it out

④

As the creme fraiche thins out, the shmoo gets thinner

⑤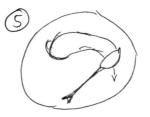

Almost done—its coming to a point

⑥

The finished shmoo!

My great-grandmother Rosalie would often serve a wedge of frittata to start a meal. I like to serve it with some greens, and sometimes I'll drizzle it with a bit of Salsa Piccante (page 162) or Bagna Cauda (page 29).

BROCCOLI RABE & POTATO FRITTATA

14 extra-large eggs

Sea salt, preferably Halen Môn (see Sources), and freshly ground black pepper

2 tbsp pure olive oil

2 Yukon gold potatoes, unpeeled, sliced ¼ inch (6 mm) thick

2 cloves garlic, sliced lengthwise into thin slivers

1 bunch broccoli rabe, tough stems removed, leaves cut crosswise into ½-inch (12-mm) pieces

¼ cup (2 fl oz/60 ml) extra-virgin olive oil

¼ cup (1 oz/30 g) toasted coarse bread crumbs

If desired, prepare a hot fire in an outdoor grill. Place a deep, 9-inch (23-cm) cast-iron skillet on the hot grill rack and leave it to pre-heat, or, heat on the stove top over medium-high heat.

In a large bowl, whisk the eggs until blended and season with salt and pepper. Pour the pure olive oil into the preheated pan and swirl to coat the bottom and sides. Layer the potato slices in the pan and cook until golden on the underside, about 3 minutes. Flip the potatoes and continue to cook until the second side is lightly golden, about 3 minutes longer. Add the garlic to the pan and stir to mix. Then add enough broccoli rabe to fill the pan, stir, and allow it to cook down until there is room to add more. Continue adding the broccoli rabe and cooking it down until all of it has been incorporated and has cooked down, 4–5 minutes total.

Stir in the extra-virgin oil and then pour in the eggs. Move the pan to a cooler area of the grill, or reduce the heat to medium-low. Using a heat-resistant rubber spatula, gently move the eggs around the pan for about 1 minute. Cover and cook for 6 minutes. Uncover and spread the bread crumbs evenly over the top. Re-cover and cook until the frittata is firm, 4–5 minutes longer.

Remove the pan from the heat and let cool for about 3 minutes. Run a butter knife around the inside edge of the pan to loosen the sides of the frittata. Invert a large flat plate over the pan, and holding the plate and the pan together, flip them to release the frittata onto the plate. Lift off the pan and serve the frittata warm or at room temperature, cut into wedges.

SERVES 10

Make this traditional Piedmontese dish at the height of spring, when all of the season's vegetables are overflowing the bins at the farmers' market. For the "hot bath," I have mixed olive oil and the region's celebrated Barolo. The wine gives the sauce depth while still allowing the vegetables to be the star.

BAROLO BAGNA CAUDA

1 bottle (24 fl oz/750 ml) Barolo or Cabernet Sauvignon, preferably from Napa Valley

1 cup (8 fl oz/250 ml) extra-virgin olive oil

½ cup (4 fl oz/125 ml) olive oil

2 salt-packed anchovies, soaked in cold water for 15–20 minutes, drained, filleted, and rinsed

¼ cup (2 oz/60 g) marinated white anchovy fillets

3 cloves garlic, coarsely chopped

Finely grated zest and juice of 1 lemon

Kosher salt and freshly ground black pepper

Small spring vegetables for dipping, such as young carrots, celery hearts, spring onions, radishes with tops, endive spears, blanched pole beans, and baby fennel

Pour the wine into a nonreactive saucepan, place over medium-high heat, bring to a boil, and cook until reduced by half. Set aside to cool.

In a blender, combine the reduced wine, both olive oils, both types of anchovy, the garlic, and the lemon zest and juice and process until smooth. Season to taste with salt and pepper.

To serve, return the mixture to the saucepan and reheat over medium-low heat until warm. Pour into a warmed heatproof serving bowl and accompany with the vegetables for dipping. If desired, keep the mixture warm by placing it on a stand set over a tea light or small sterno.

SERVES 10

Sunchokes, artichokes, and sunflowers are all in the same botanical family, so why not serve them all together? I like the mix of textures—creamy, crisp, and crunchy. The tart vinaigrette binds the three elements nicely. You can think of agliata as bread crumb salsa. It's a versatile addition to many different dishes.

SUNCHOKES, ARTICHOKES & SUNFLOWERS

½ lemon

12 baby artichokes

Kosher salt and freshly ground black pepper

4 bay leaves

4 fresh thyme sprigs

¼ cup (1 oz/30 g) sunflower seeds

1 tbsp extra-virgin olive oil

12 sunchokes, scrubbed

Preheat the oven to 325°F (165°C).

Fill a large bowl three-fourths full with cold water and squeeze in the juice of the lemon half. Working with 1 artichoke at a time, pull back the outer leaves, one at a time, until they break at the base. Continue removing the leaves in the same manner until you reach the innermost yellow leaves with prickly tips. Cut across the artichoke just below the tip and discard the tip, and then trim off all but 1 inch (2.5 cm) of the stem. Using a paring knife or vegetable peeler, trim off the outer layer of the stem and trim the base to remove any dark green bits. Drop the trimmed artichoke into the lemon water and repeat with the remaining artichokes.

Remove the artichokes from the lemon water, reserving the water, and pat dry. Cut each artichoke in half lengthwise and place cut-side down in a single layer in a shallow roasting pan. Season with ¼ teaspoon salt, several grinds of pepper, the bay, and the thyme. Add 2 tablespoons of the lemon water, then cover the pan with parchment paper and then with aluminum foil. Roast the artichokes until tender when pierced with a knife tip, about 45 minutes. Remove from the oven, uncover, and let cool to room temperature. Leave the oven set at 325°F (165°C).

In a small bowl, toss the sunflower seeds with the 1 tablespoon olive oil, coating evenly. Spread the seeds in a small shallow pan, place in the oven, and roast until golden, 2–3 minutes. Let cool completely.

Using a mandoline or other vegetable slicer, cut each sunchoke lengthwise into paper-thin slices. Place the cooled artichokes

2 tbsp Lemon Vinaigrette (page 160)

1 cup (1½ oz/45 g) sunflower sprouts

¼ cup (¼ oz/7 g) loosely packed fresh flat-leaf parsley leaves

AGLIATA

5 tbsp (3 fl oz/80 ml) extra-virgin olive oil

½ cup (2 oz/60 g) coarse dried bread crumbs

Finely grated zest of 1 lemon

2 tbsp chopped fresh flat-leaf parsley

2 tbsp chopped fresh mint

1 tbsp very finely chopped garlic

Kosher salt and freshly ground black pepper

in a bowl, drizzle with most of the vinaigrette, and toss to coat evenly. Add the sunflower sprouts and sunchoke slices and toss gently to coat. Add the parsley and toasted sunflower seeds and toss gently. Taste and adjust the seasoning.

To make the *agliata,* in a sauté pan over medium heat, warm 1 tablespoon of the olive oil. Add the bread crumbs and sauté until crunchy, about 5 minutes. Add the lemon zest, parsley, and mint and sauté to cook the herbs lightly. Transfer the contents of the pan to a rimmed baking sheet, spreading it evenly, and let cool. In a bowl, combine the cooled bread crumb mixture, garlic, and the remaining 4 tablespoons (2 fl oz/60 ml) extra-virgin olive oil and toss to mix. Season with salt and pepper.

To serve, divide the salad evenly among individual plates, taking care to divide the separate elements evenly. Top each salad with the *agliata,* drizzle with the remaining vinaigrette, and finish with a generous grind of pepper. Serve right away.

SERVES 4

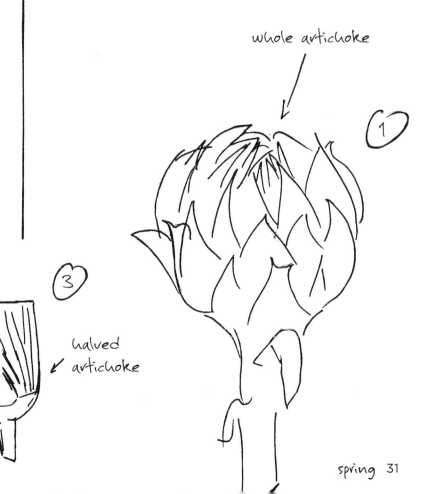

whole artichoke

cleaned artichoke

halved artichoke

I like to use asparagus in as many ways as possible. Both raw and cooked asparagus pair well with earthy potatoes and salty caviar. If they are available, use white and purple spears to really make the dish soigné.

ASPARAGUS, SPRING POTATOES, CRÈME FRAÎCHE & CAVIAR

CRÈME FRAÎCHE DRESSING

2 tbsp crème fraîche

1 tsp extra-virgin olive oil

Finely grated zest of ¼ lemon

Pinch of kosher salt and freshly ground black pepper

2 tsp minced fresh chives

8–12 small fingerling potatoes

16 jumbo asparagus spears

2 tbsp extra-virgin olive oil

1 tsp fresh lemon juice

Sea salt, preferably Halen Môn (see Sources), and freshly ground black pepper

1 oz (30 g) caviar

Fresh chervil leaves

To make the dressing, in a bowl, gently mix together the crème fraîche, oil, lemon zest, salt, and chives. Cover and refrigerate.

In a saucepan, cover the potatoes with salted water, bring to a boil, reduce the heat to a simmer, and cook until just tender when pierced with a knife, 10–15 minutes. Drain the potatoes, let cool until they can be handled, and then peel. Let cool completely.

Snap off the tough base from each asparagus, and trim the ends even. Using a vegetable peeler, peel 6 of the asparagus spears to within about 1 inch (2.5 cm) of the tip. Leave the remaining 10 spears unpeeled. Bring a large saucepan three-fourths full of salted water to a boil. Add the peeled spears and 6 of the unpeeled spears to the boiling water, count slowly to ten, and then immediately remove from the water and place on a rimmed baking sheet to cool. Do not immerse in cold water.

Transfer the cooled asparagus to a shallow bowl, dress with the olive oil, lemon juice, salt, and pepper, and arrange on a platter. In a separate bowl, season the potatoes with salt and pepper and then toss with the crème fraîche dressing. Scatter the potatoes over the platter and drizzle any dressing in the bottom of the bowl over the top. Using the vegetable peeler, thinly slice the remaining 4 raw asparagus spears lengthwise, capturing the slices in the bowl in which the blanched asparagus were dressed. Drape the raw asparagus slices attractively over the potatoes and asparagus on the platter. Top with small piles of the caviar and scatter over a few chervil leaves. Serve right away.

SERVES 4

I have often wondered who was the first person to realize that eating an artichoke was a good idea. This recipe offers a quick and easy way to taste the true flavor of the artichoke by using it raw, cut into paper-thin slices.

ARTICHOKES, MINT & LEMON

1 lemon, plus 3 tbsp fresh juice

10 baby artichokes

3 tbsp extra-virgin olive oil

Kosher salt and freshly ground black pepper

½ lb (250 g) arugula leaves, preferably wild

¼ cup (⅓ oz/10 g) torn fresh mint leaves

Wedge of Parmigiano-Reggiano cheese for shaving

Fill a large bowl three-fourths full with cold water and squeeze in the juice of the lemon. Working with 1 artichoke at a time, pull back the outer leaves one at a time until they break at the base. Continue removing the leaves in the same manner until you reach the innermost yellow leaves with prickly tips. Cut across the artichoke just below the tip and discard the tip, and then trim off all but 1 inch (2.5 cm) of the stem. Using a paring knife or vegetable peeler, trim off the outer layer of the stem and trim the base to remove any dark green bits. Drop the trimmed artichoke into the lemon water and repeat with the remaining artichokes.

Remove the artichokes from the lemon water and pat dry. Using a mandoline or other vegetable slicer, cut each artichoke lengthwise into paper-thin slices. Transfer the artichokes to a bowl, drizzle with the 3 tablespoons lemon juice and the olive oil, toss to coat, and then season with salt and pepper. Add the arugula and mint and toss gently.

Divide the salad among individual plates, spreading it flat. Using a vegetable peeler, shave a few Parmigiano-Reggiano curls over each salad. Serve right away.

SERVES 4

This is not your grandmother's three-bean salad! Look on this recipe as a template that you can fashion with as many different types of beans as you like. I think that the more colors and textures you have the better. I especially like the crispiness of the radish mixed with the creaminess of the cannellini beans.

BEAN & RADISH SALAD

CANNELLINI BEANS

1½ cups (10½ oz/330 g) dried cannellini beans

1 yellow onion

1 celery rib, halved

1 carrot

Kosher salt and freshly ground black pepper

Extra-virgin olive oil

1 lb (500 g) mixed pole beans, such as Romano, yellow and purple wax, Dragon Tongue, and Blue Lake

8 red radishes, trimmed and cut into slices ¼ inch (6 mm) thick

1 red onion, thinly sliced into rings

Zinfandel Vinaigrette (page 160)

Kosher salt and freshly ground black pepper

⅓ cup (⅓ oz/10 g) small fresh basil leaves, preferably Piccolo Fino Verde

Pick over the beans, discarding any grit or misshapen beans. Rinse the beans under cold running water, transfer to a large pot, add water to cover by 2 inches (5 cm), and let stand for at least 4 hours or up to overnight.

Drain the beans and return them to the pot. Add the onion, celery, carrot, and water to cover by 2 inches (5 cm). Place over medium heat, bring to a simmer, and cook until tender, about 2 hours. The timing will depend on the age of the beans.

Remove from the heat and let the cannellini beans cool in the cooking liquid. Remove and discard the onion, celery, and carrot. Season the beans with salt and pepper and a big splash of olive oil. Cover and refrigerate overnight before serving.

Have ready a large bowl of salted ice water. Bring a large saucepan three-fourths full of salted water to a boil over high heat. Add the pole beans and cook until tender-crisp, about 2 minutes. Drain immediately and immerse in the ice water to cool completely. Drain and pat dry.

Drain the cannellini beans well, transfer to a large bowl, and add the pole beans, radishes, and onion. Drizzle with the vinaigrette, season with salt and pepper, and toss to mix. Sprinkle in the basil and taste and adjust the seasoning if needed. Divide among chilled individual plates and serve.

SERVES 10

In spring in California, the wild boar population explodes and the animals can be seen rummaging through gardens and vineyards. Pickling the meat in vinegar alters its texture, making it tender enough to slice thinly and serve cold. The mixed-herb pesto balances the acidity of the pickled meat.

PICKLED BOAR, HERB PESTO, GRILLED ONIONS & PINE NUTS

1 boneless boar shoulder
(see Sources), 3–4 lb
(1.5–2 kg)

1 *each* yellow onion, carrot, and fennel bulb, each cut in half

1 head garlic, halved crosswise

12 fresh thyme sprigs, crushed

1 tbsp *each* fennel seeds, coriander seeds, and black peppercorns

2 bay leaves

Good-quality red wine vinegar

MARINADE

1 cup (8 fl oz/250 ml) balsamic vinegar

1 cup (8 fl oz/250 ml) red wine vinegar

12 fresh thyme sprigs

3 cloves garlic, unpeeled, crushed

Extra-virgin olive oil

Kosher salt and freshly ground black pepper

(continued)

Trim the shoulder of any visible sinew, gristle, and fat. Following the natural seams of the meat, cut the shoulder into 4 or 5 odd-sized pieces.

In a large, nonreactive pot, combine the boar pieces, onion, carrot, fennel bulb, garlic, thyme, fennel seeds, coriander seeds, peppercorns, and bay. Add water to cover, measuring as you go. When the boar is covered, add 1 cup (8 fl oz/250 ml) vinegar to the pot for every 4 qt (4 l) water. Place over high heat, bring to a boil, and immediately reduce the heat to a simmer. Cook uncovered, skimming away any impurities that rise to the surface, until the meat is fork-tender, about 2 hours.

Transfer the meat pieces, keeping them whole, to a glass or ceramic bowl or other nonreactive container in which they fit snugly. Discard the braising liquid.

To make the marinade, in another ceramic or glass bowl, stir together both vinegars, the thyme (crush it slightly first), garlic, and a splash of extra-virgin olive oil and season with salt and pepper. Pour the marinade over the warm meat, shifting the meat as needed to immerse all of the pieces completely in the marinade. Refrigerate uncovered, rotating the meat pieces as needed to ensure that the marinade reaches all of the surfaces, until the meat is no longer warm. Cover with plastic wrap and marinate in the refrigerator for 24 hours.

Remove the meat from the refrigerator and bring to room temperature; this will take about an hour or so. Meanwhile, prepare the grilled onions and the pesto.
(continued)

GRILLED RED ONIONS

Zinfandel vinegar

Pure olive oil

Kosher salt and freshly ground black pepper

1 red onion, cut crosswise into thin slices

HERB PESTO

1 cup (1 oz/30 g) fresh flat-leaf parsley leaves

1 cup (1 oz/30 g) fresh basil leaves

1 cup (1 oz/30 g) fresh mint leaves

2 cloves garlic

¼ cup (1½ oz/45 g) pine nuts, toasted

2-oz (60-g) piece Parmigiano-Reggiano cheese, broken into pieces

1½ cups (12 fl oz/375 ml) extra-virgin olive oil

Kosher salt and freshly ground black pepper

1 cup (1 oz/30 g) arugula leaves, preferably wild

Extra-virgin olive oil as needed

¼ cup (1½ oz/45 g) pine nuts, toasted

To prepare the onions, in a shallow bowl, whisk together a splash each of the vinegar and olive oil and season to taste with salt and pepper. Add the onion slices and turn to coat lightly and evenly. Let stand for 1 hour before grilling.

Prepare a medium fire in a charcoal or gas grill. When the fire is ready, arrange the onion slices on the grill rack and grill, turning once, until etched with grill marks on both sides and tender, about 3 minutes on each side. Transfer to a plate and let cool.

To make the pesto, have ready a large bowl of salted ice water. Bring a saucepan three-fourths full of salted water to a boil over high heat. Add the parsley, basil, and mint, blanch for 20 seconds, and then drain and immediately immerse in the ice water to cool completely. Scoop out the cooled herbs, squeeze to remove the excess moisture, and chop coarsely.

In a blender, combine the herbs in 3 or 4 layers alternately with the garlic, pine nuts, Parmigiano-Reggiano, and olive oil. Process until relatively smooth, but still with some texture. Transfer to a bowl and season to taste with salt and pepper.

To serve, spread the pesto in a circle on a large platter, or on individual plates, making the layer thin enough so that the plate is visible through it. Remove the boar from the marinade and reserve a little of the marinade. Cut the boar against the grain into slices ⅛ inch (3 mm) thick. Arrange the slices in an overlapping pattern across the platter or plates on top of the pesto. In a bowl, combine the arugula, grilled onions, separated into rings, and a splash each of extra-virgin olive oil and the marinade and toss to coat evenly. Arrange the arugula mixture on the platter or plates next to or on top of the boar slices and sprinkle with the pine nuts. Finish with a drizzle of olive oil and serve right away.

SERVES 8

I always like to have a nice brothy soup in my back pocket for this time of year. The sweet green garlic balances well with the richness of the poached egg, providing the comfort you need on a day when you hoped to go out and enjoy the sun but Mother Nature dealt you a different hand.

GREEN GARLIC BRODO, POACHED EGG & FRIED BREAD

2 bunches green garlic (about 12 stalks total), root ends and tough tops trimmed

2 tbsp extra-virgin olive oil

1 head mature garlic, split crosswise

¼ cup (2 fl oz/60 ml) dry white wine

8 cups (64 fl oz/2 l) Chicken Stock (page 164)

1 bay leaf

4-by-1-inch (10-by-2.5-cm) piece Parmigiano-Reggiano cheese rind

Kosher salt and freshly ground black pepper

½ cup (4 fl oz/125 ml) pure olive oil

3 cups (6 oz/185 g) torn coarse country bread

1–2 tsp seasoned rice or distilled white vinegar

6 large eggs

Cut the green leaves on each garlic stalk crosswise into thin rings. Then, cut the white bottoms lengthwise into julienne. In a saucepan over medium heat, warm the extra-virgin olive oil. Add the split garlic head and cook until golden brown on all sides, about 3 minutes. Add all of the green garlic and sauté until translucent, 6–8 minutes. Add the wine and cook, stirring to dislodge any browned bits from the pan bottom, until the wine has evaporated, about 3 minutes. Add the stock, bay, and cheese rind, bring to a simmer, and cook to blend the flavors, about 10 minutes. Season to taste with salt and pepper and keep warm off the heat.

In a sauté pan over high heat, warm the pure olive oil until ripples appear. Add the bread and fry, turning as needed, until golden brown, about 5 minutes. Using a slotted spoon, transfer the bread to paper towels to drain and season with salt and pepper.

Pour water to a depth of 2 inches (5 cm) into a large, deep sauté pan. Add the vinegar, bring to a boil over high heat, and reduce the heat until the water is just under a boil. One at a time and working quickly, break each egg into a small cup and gently slip the egg into the water. Remove from the heat, cover the pan, and let stand until the whites are firm and the yolks are glazed but still liquid, about 4 minutes.

Meanwhile, reheat the soup until piping hot and ladle into warmed shallow individual bowls. Using a slotted spoon, transfer each egg to a bowl, placing it in the center. Divide the bread evenly among the bowls, scattering it over the top, and serve.

SERVES 6

There is no better way to eat an egg with a runny yolk than on a nice piece of grilled bread. Topping the egg with briny anchovy fillets and fresh herbs makes a great bite, and the bread turns the whole package into an extraordinary handheld snack.

EGG & ANCHOVY CROSTINI

2 extra-large eggs

8-inch (20-cm) baguette, split lengthwise

1 tbsp extra-virgin olive oil, plus more for drizzling

Sea salt, preferably Halen Môn (see Sources), and freshly ground black pepper

1 lemon

1 tbsp roughly chopped fresh flat-leaf parsley

1 tbsp fresh chive batons (½-inch/12-mm lengths)

4–8 marinated white anchovy fillets

Have ready a bowl filled with salted ice water (the salt helps the shells come off the eggs more easily). Bring a saucepan three-fourths full of water to a boil over high heat. Add the eggs and cook for 6½ minutes. Scoop the eggs out the water and immediately immerse them in the ice water to cool completely, about 5 minutes. Peel the cooled eggs, being careful to keep them intact, and reserve.

Preheat a stove-top grill pan over medium heat. Brush the baguette lengths on both sides with the 1 tablespoon olive oil and then season on both sides with salt and pepper. Grill the bread, turning once, until etched with grill marks and crisp on both sides, 2–3 minutes on each side.

Rub the cut side of each toasted baguette length with the whole lemon, releasing the natural oils of the zest to flavor the bread. Then, finely grate the lemon zest. In a small bowl, mix the parsley and chives.

Cut each baguette length in half crosswise on a slight diagonal and arrange on a platter. Cut each egg in half lengthwise and place an egg half, cut side up, on each piece of bread. Season the eggs with salt and pepper. Top each egg half with 1 or 2 anchovy fillets and some of the herb mixture, then finish with a drizzle of olive oil, and sprinkle with the lemon zest. Serve right away.

SERVES 4

As spring progresses, fava beans grow larger and have to be shelled twice, which means that you want the rest of the dish to be easy. Here is a perfect combination of the season, featuring sweet, sour, salty, and rich ingredients all together.

FAVA BEANS, STRAWBERRIES & PECORINO

2 cups (14 oz/440 g) shelled young, tender fava beans (about 2 lb/1 kg in the pod)

2 cups (8 oz/250 g) strawberries, stemmed and quartered lengthwise

Vanilla salt, preferably Halen Môn (see Sources), and freshly ground black pepper

1 bunch arugula (about 4 oz/125 g), preferably wild, tough stems removed

1–2 tbsp Balsamic Vinaigrette (page 160)

Wedge of young pecorino cheese for shaving

Bring a large saucepan three-fourths full of salted water to a boil over high heat. Have ready a large bowl filled with salted ice water. Add the fava beans to the boiling water, blanch for 1 minute, drain, and immediately immerse in the ice water to cool completely. Drain the fava beans and then pinch off the outer skin from each larger bean by pinching the bean at one end. The skins on the smaller beans are neither tough nor bitter and can remain intact. Place the beans in a bowl. Discard the outer skins.

Add the strawberries to the fava beans and season to taste with vanilla salt and pepper. Add the arugula, drizzle with the vinaigrette to taste, and toss to mix evenly. Taste and adjust the seasoning with salt and pepper.

Transfer the salad to a platter or divide among individual plates. Using a vegetable peeler, shave a few pecorino curls over the top. Serve right away.

SERVES 6

Serving roasted lamb in the spring is iconic and I like to keep the preparation simple. Anchovy and mint are classic Italian pairings, so I decided to combine them in a compound butter that can be made in advance and put on the meat at the last minute.

SPRING LAMB, ANCHOVY & MINT

2 boneless lamb loins, about 1 lb (500 g) each, trimmed of excess fat

Kosher salt and freshly ground black pepper

2 tbsp olive oil

1 bunch fresh mint

1 head garlic, split crosswise

6 tbsp (3 oz/90 g) Anchovy Butter (page 163)

Preheat the oven to 425°F (220°C). Season the lamb loins with salt and pepper.

Heat a heavy cast-iron pan over high heat until very hot and then add the olive oil. When the oil is hot, add the lamb loins, mint, and garlic and sear the lamb loins, basting them with the olive oil and flipping them once, until golden brown on both sides, about 5 minutes total. Transfer the pan to the oven and roast for about 15 minutes. To test for doneness, insert an instant-read thermometer into the thickest part of a loin; it should register 125°F (52°C) for medium-rare or 130°F (54°C) for medium (before resting).

Transfer the lamb to a cutting board, tent with aluminum foil, and let rest for 10 minutes.

To serve, slice the loins against the grain and arrange on warmed individual plates. Top each serving with a slice of the anchovy butter and serve right away. If desired, serve with the mint and garlic, or discard.

SERVES 6

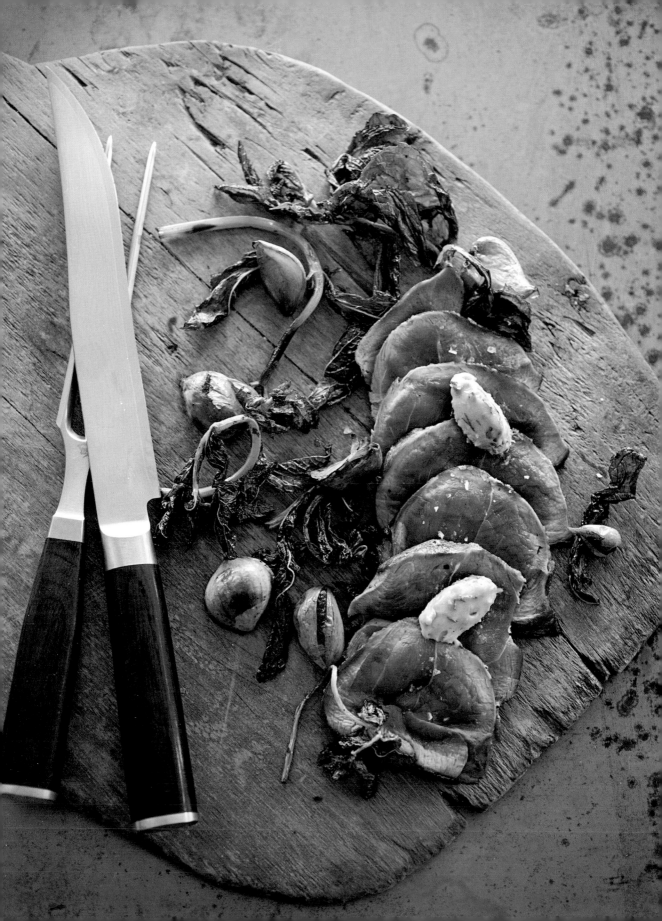

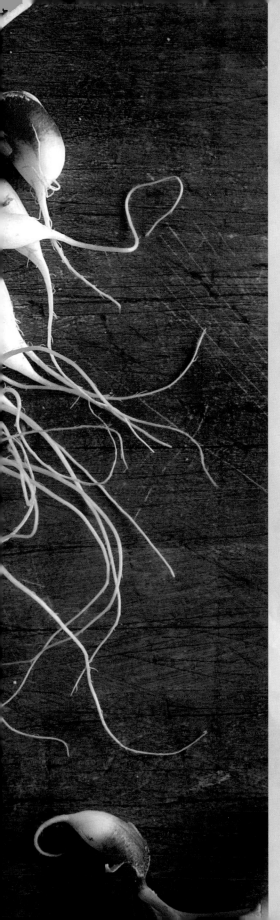

summer

Castelvetranos are like the jack-of-all trades in the olive world: they're good raw, cooked, and pressed into oil. Roasting them and cherry tomatoes along with tomato leaves brings out amazing flavor and aromas (the stories of tomato leaves being poisonous aren't true). To serve larger groups, multiply the ingredients and use a larger pan.

ROASTED CASTELVETRANO OLIVES & CHERRY TOMATOES

¾ cup (4 oz/125 g) Castelvetrano or other mild, salt-brined green olives

1 cup (6 oz/185 g) cherry tomatoes, in assorted colors

4 cloves garlic, crushed

3 tbsp extra-virgin olive oil, preferably Castelvetrano

5 organic tomato leaves

Grilled or toasted coarse country bread for dipping

Preheat the oven to 450°F (230°C).

In a bowl, toss together the olives, tomatoes, garlic, olive oil, and tomato leaves to mix well. Transfer to an attractive broiler-safe sauté pan or baking dish and roast until softened, about 15 minutes. Turn the oven setting to broil, move the dish to the top oven rack, and broil until the olives and tomatoes are blistered, about 1 minute.

Place the dish on a trivet on the table. Serve right away with the bread alongside.

SERVES 2

tomato leaves

In summer, when local peaches are in full swing, I grill them; the caramelized juices paired with smokiness is addictive. I combine them with a little sweet, mild Gorgonzola dolcelatte, bitter dandelion greens, and fresh mint, making the perfect summertime salad.

GRILLED PEACHES, GORGONZOLA & DANDELION GREENS

2 firm but ripe peaches, preferably white peaches, halved and pitted

Kosher salt and coarsely ground black pepper

2 tbsp extra-virgin olive oil, plus more for drizzling

2 tbsp balsamic vinegar

1 small red onion, sliced crosswise ¼ inch (6 mm) thick

4 cups (4 oz/125 g) baby dandelion greens

¼ cup (¼ oz/7 g) fresh mint leaves

1–2 tbsp Balsamic Vinaigrette (page 160)

4 tbsp (1½ oz/45 g) crumbled Gorgonzola *dolcelatte* cheese

Place the peach halves in a shallow bowl, season with salt and pepper, add 1 tablespoon each of the olive oil and vinegar, and toss to coat evenly. Set aside to marinate while you prepare the other ingredients and the grill.

Prepare a medium fire in a charcoal or gas grill.

In a bowl, toss the onion slices with the remaining 1 tablespoon each of the olive oil and vinegar, season lightly with salt and pepper, and set aside.

When the fire is ready, put the peaches, cut side down, on the grill rack and cook slowly, turning once, until evenly caramelized on both sides, about 4 minutes on each side. While the peaches are grilling, place the marinated onion slices on the grill rack and grill, turning once, until etched with grill marks and nicely caramelized on both sides, about 1 minute on each side.

To serve, cut each warm peach half in half and place the pieces, cut side up, in the center of an individual plate. In a bowl, combine the dandelion greens, warm grilled onions, separated into rings, and mint. Drizzle with the vinaigrette and toss to coat evenly. Season with salt and pepper, toss again, and divide evenly among the plates, placing the salad on top of the peach halves. Garnish each salad with Gorgonzola, drizzle lightly with olive oil, and grind pepper over the top. Serve right away.

SERVES 4

Sardines are my favorite fish because they pack so much flavor. At the restaurant, I serve them in many ways. Once you eat them, you'll appreciate why sardines are a favorite snack of bluefin tuna.

GRILLED SARDINES & SALSA VERDE

3 lemons

8 fresh sardines, cleaned

Kosher salt and freshly ground black pepper

¾ cup (6 fl oz/180 ml) Salsa Verde (page 162)

Extra-virgin olive oil for drizzling

Prepare a medium-hot fire in a charcoal or gas grill.

Meanwhile, finely grate the zest from 1 lemon and then juice the lemon. Halve the remaining 2 lemons crosswise and reserve. Season the sardines with salt, pepper, and the lemon zest and juice, turning to coat evenly. Let stand while the grill gets hot.

Arrange the sardines on the grill rack, positioning the heads at 2 o'clock, and grill for 1½ minutes. Reposition the sardines so the heads are at 11 o'clock and continue to grill for 1½ minutes to create crosshatch grill marks. Carefully turn the sardines over, once again positioning the heads at 2 o'clock, and grill for 1½ minutes. Then shift the heads to the 11 o'clock position and continue to grill until done, 1½ minutes longer. The flesh of the sardines should be opaque when pierced with a knife. When you turn over the sardines, put the lemon halves, cut side down, on the grill rack and grill until nicely etched with grill marks, 2½–3 minutes.

Transfer the sardines and lemon halves to individual plates, putting 1 sardine and 1 lemon half on each plate. Spoon 3 tablespoons of the salsa over each sardine, drizzle lightly with olive oil, and serve right away, encouraging your guests to squeeze the lemon half over the fish before eating.

SERVES 4

Pappa al pomodoro literally translates to bread and tomato. I turn the classic Italian thick soup into a more refined plate by making a crispy French toast-style dish. I sear tomato-soaked bread until it caramelizes on the outside but is still soft on the inside and then top it with a fresh tomato salad.

PAPPA AL POMODORO (VERSION 2.0)

4 slices coarse country bread or baguette slices, 1 inch (2.5 cm) thick

8 very ripe red heirloom tomatoes, about 2 lb (1 kg) total weight, cut into chunks

4 cloves garlic, crushed

1 cup (1 oz/30 g) fresh basil leaves

Kosher salt and freshly ground black pepper

CHERRY TOMATO SALAD

2 cups (12 oz/375 g) cherry tomatoes, in assorted colors, large ones cut in half

¼ cup (¼ oz/7 g) mixed fresh opal and Genovese basil leaves, torn

¼ cup (1 oz/30 g) julienned red onion

Kosher salt and freshly ground black pepper

1 tbsp Zinfandel Vinaigrette (page 160)

½ cup (4 fl oz/125 ml) extra-virgin olive oil, preferably Coratina brand (see Sources)

If you have a gas oven, the night before you plan to serve the dish, arrange the bread slices on a rimmed baking sheet, place in the oven, and leave there overnight. The bread will dry from the heat of the pilot light. (Alternatively, toast the bread in a toaster oven. Let the bread slices cool and then let stand overnight at room temperature until completely dried out.) This step is important, or the bread will fall apart during cooking.

In a blender or food processor, combine the tomatoes, garlic, basil, 1 teaspoon salt, and 1 teaspoon pepper and process until smooth. Transfer the purée to a glass or ceramic baking dish, submerge the bread slices in the tomato mixture, and let stand for 5 minutes.

Meanwhile, make the cherry tomato salad. In a bowl, combine the cherry tomatoes, basil, and onion and season with salt and pepper. Drizzle with the vinaigrette and toss to coat evenly.

In a large nonstick sauté pan over medium heat, warm the olive oil. When the oil is hot, remove the bread slices from the purée and add to the pan. Cook until nicely seared on the underside, about 3 minutes. Flip the slices and cook on the second side until nicely seared and hot throughout, about 3 minutes longer.

Transfer the seared bread to a warmed platter or divide among individual plates. Arrange the tomato salad on top of the bread slices. Serve right away.

SERVES 4

Cucumbers are excellent vehicles for many flavors, but if treated properly, they also display great individuality. I use three different varieties here to show off their distinctive flavors. The dusting of bottarga imparts just enough fish flavor to give the dish a nice briny quality.

CUCUMBERS, RADISHES & BOTTARGA

1 small torpedo onion

1 lemon cucumber

1 Armenian cucumber

1 Mediterranean cucumber

12 assorted radishes such as French breakfast, Red Globe, and Easter Egg

Kosher salt and freshly ground black pepper

2 tbsp Zinfandel Vinaigrette (page 160)

⅓ cup (⅓ oz/10 g) fresh flat-leaf parsley leaves

Grey mullet *bottarga* (see Sources) for grating

Fill a bowl with salted ice water. Thinly slice the onion crosswise, separate the slices into rings, and immerse the rings in the ice water. Let stand for 5 minutes.

Trim both ends from the cucumbers and radishes. Quarter the lemon cucumber lengthwise. Using a mandoline or other vegetable slicer or a sharp knife, cut the Armenian and Mediterranean cucumbers and large radishes crosswise into slices ⅛ inch (3 mm) thick. If desired, leave small radishes whole. In a bowl, combine the cucumbers and radishes and season with salt and pepper.

Drain the onion rings, pat dry, and add to the bowl with the cucumbers and radishes. Drizzle a little of the vinaigrette over the vegetables, toss to coat, and then taste and adjust the seasoning if needed.

Divide the cucumber mixture evenly among chilled individual plates. Dress the parsley with the vinaigrette left in the bottom of the bowl that held the cucumbers and scatter over the salad. Using a Microplane or other fine rasp grater, grate a light dusting of the *bottarga* over each salad. Serve right away.

SERVES 6

bottarga di muggine

Some authorities claim this dish originated in Italy and others say it's Italian-American. What we know for sure is that fra diavolo means "from the devil," which translates to some serious chile heat. Breaking from tradition, I serve the claws cooked and the tail raw to showcase the rich, buttery quality of the lobster.

LOBSTER CRUDO FRA DIAVOLO

3½ qt (3.5 l) Court Bouillon (page 163)

2 live lobsters, about 2 lb (1 kg) each

2 cloves garlic, very finely chopped (about 1 tsp)

1 red Fresno chile, sliced into paper-thin rings

1 tbsp capers

2 tbsp fresh flat-leaf parsley leaves, torn

2 tbsp fresh mint leaves, torn

2 cups (12 oz/375 g) cherry tomatoes, in assorted colors, halved

1 tsp fresh lemon juice

1 tsp finely grated lemon zest

1 tsp extra-virgin olive oil

1 serrano chile, sliced into paper-thin rings

1 tsp ground Aleppo pepper

Sea salt, preferably Halen Môn (see Sources), and freshly ground black pepper

Place a serving platter in the refrigerator to chill. In a large, tall pot, bring the court bouillon to a boil over high heat. While the liquid is heating, place the lobsters on a work surface. Working with one lobster at a time, plunge the tip of a sharp knife straight down right behind the lobster's eyes to kill it. Twist off the lobster claws and knuckles and set aside. Then twist off the tail from the body. Run a bamboo skewer lengthwise through the tail of each lobster to keep it straight as it cooks.

Prepare a large salted ice-water bath. When the court bouillon is boiling, add the lobster tails and let them cook for 3 minutes. Using tongs, immediately transfer the tails to the ice water. Return the court bouillon to a boil, add the lobster claws and knuckles to the boiling liquid, and boil until dark red and fully cooked, about 5 minutes, then immediately transfer them to the ice water to cool completely.

Remove the tails from the ice water and drain. Turn the tail belly side up on a work surface, and using kitchen shears, carefully cut through the membrane on both sides of the shell and gently pull away the membrane. Lift the tail meat away from the shell, keeping it in one piece. Repeat with the second lobster. Reserve the tail meat.

Transfer the cooled claws and knuckles to a work surface. Using the shears or a lobster cracker, remove the meat from the claws and knuckles and reserve. Reserve all of the shells and remaining pieces for another use, such as lobster stock, or discard. (continued)

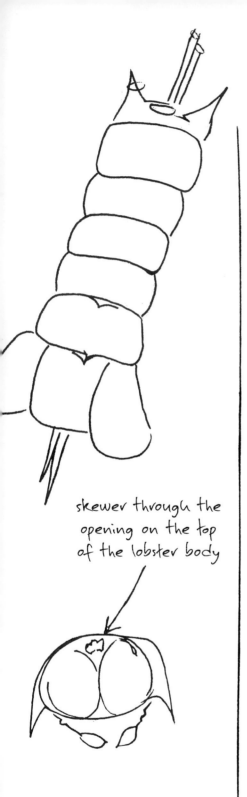

skewer through the
opening on the top
of the lobster body

Cut the tail meat on the diagonal into slices ¼ inch (6 mm) thick. You should have 18 slices. Arrange the slices on the chilled platter or individual plates. Put any bits of tail meat into a bowl. If desired, reserve 2 of the claw pieces for garnish. Cut the remaining claw and knuckle meat into bite-size pieces. Add to the bowl with the tail meat. Add the garlic, Fresno chile, capers, parsley, mint, and cherry tomatoes to the bowl.

In a small bowl, whisk together the lemon juice and zest, and olive oil until emulsified. Add the serrano chile, Aleppo pepper, salt, and black pepper mix well to make a dressing. Drizzle about half of the dressing over the lobster meat mixture in the bowl, and toss to coat evenly.

Arrange the dressed lobster meat on the platter with the sliced raw lobster, or place it on top of the sliced lobster on the plates, dividing it evenly. Drizzle the remaining dressing over the sliced lobster meat. Garnish the platter with the reserved claw pieces, if using. Serve right away.

SERVES 6

I like the simplicity of this salad, with each element—
eggplant, onion, chile—nicely blending with the others.
You can prepare the dish a day in advance, cover, and
refrigerate it and then let it come to room temperature
before serving. Leftover dressing can be used to flavor
sliced tomatoes or as a marinade for chicken.

CHARRED EGGPLANT, SUMMER ONIONS & CHILE

CHILE DRESSING

2 red Fresno chiles

2 dried chiles, seeded

1 tsp hot *pimentón de la Vera* (see Sources)

Kosher salt

1 cup (8 fl oz/250 ml) extra-virgin olive oil

3 tbsp Cabernet vinegar

2 large globe eggplants

1 tbsp extra-virgin olive oil

Kosher salt and freshly ground black pepper

3 small summer onions, thinly sliced

1 cup (1 oz/30 g) arugula leaves, preferably wild

¼ cup (¼ oz/7 g) mixed fresh opal and Genovese basil leaves

Prepare a hot fire in a charcoal or gas grill.

While the grill is heating, make the dressing: In a blender, combine the Fresno chiles, dried chiles, *pimentón,* ½ teaspoon salt, and the olive oil and process until thin and smooth. Pour the dressing through a fine-mesh sieve and then stir in the vinegar.

When the fire is ready, season the whole eggplants on all sides with the 1 tablespoon olive oil, salt, and pepper. Place on the grill rack and grill, turning as needed, until the skin is charred on all sides and the flesh at the center is tender when pierced with a thin skewer, about 12 minutes. Transfer to a bowl, cover with plastic wrap, and let stand for 10 minutes, or until cool enough to handle. (The trapped steam will loosen the skins and cook the flesh a bit more.)

Trim both ends of each eggplant and peel off the skin with a paring knife. Cut each eggplant lengthwise into 6 wedges. Place the wedges in a shallow glass or ceramic bowl or dish, season with salt and pepper, and pour 2 tablespoons of the dressing over the top. Cover and marinate at room temperature for 4 hours.

Divide the eggplant wedges evenly among individual plates. In a bowl, combine the onions, arugula, and basil, drizzle with the dressing to taste, and toss to coat evenly. If there is dressing remaining, reserve it for another use. Divide the onion mixture evenly among the plates, arranging it over the eggplant wedges. Serve right away.

SERVES 4

The name of this dish is inspired by the promotional slogan that appeared on crates of California fruits shipped across the country in the decades following the completion of the first transcontinental railroad. It appears the same way on my menu at Incanto. Use this salad recipe as a template, switching out the fruits and nuts listed here for whatever looks good at the market.

"LAND OF FRUITS & NUTS"

PISTACHIO BUTTER

1 cup (4 oz/125 g) pistachio nuts

3 tbsp pistachio oil or extra-virgin olive oil

Kosher salt

¼ cup (1 oz/30 g) pistachio nuts

1 tbsp extra-virgin olive oil

Sea salt, preferably Halen Môn (see Sources), and freshly ground black pepper

3 lb (1.5 kg) heirloom tomatoes, in assorted colors

2 melons, in different varieties and preferably different colors

¼ lb (125 g) arugula leaves

¼ cup (¼ oz/7 g) fresh opal basil leaves, torn

1 serrano chile, cut into paper-thin rings

¼ cup (2 fl oz/60 ml) Zinfandel Vinaigrette (page 160)

To make the pistachio butter, preheat the oven to 350°F (180°C). Spread the pistachios on a rimmed baking sheet and roast in the oven until dry and fragrant, about 5 minutes. Let cool completely and then transfer to a blender, add the oil and a pinch of salt, and process until smooth and spreadable. Transfer to an airtight container and reserve. (The butter can be made up to 2 weeks in advance, covered, and refrigerated. Bring to room temperature before using.) Reduce the oven temperature to 325°F (165°C).

In a small bowl, toss the ¼ cup (1 oz/30 g) pistachios with the 1 tablespoon oil and a little salt, spread on the baking sheet, and roast in the oven until golden brown, about 5 minutes. Let cool.

Cut the tomatoes into different shapes and sizes, such as slices 1 inch (2.5 cm) thick and ½-inch (12-mm) wedges. Halve the melons, discard the seeds, and then peel away the skin, making sure you keep their nice round shape. Cut the melon halves into different shapes, such as crescent moons, halved crescent moons, and cubes. In a large bowl, combine the tomatoes, melons, toasted pistachios, arugula, basil, and about half of the chile rings. Drizzle with the vinaigrette and toss to coat evenly. Season with salt and pepper, toss again, and then taste and adjust the seasonings.

To serve, put 1 tablespoon of the pistachio butter on 4 different areas of a large platter, and using the back of a spoon, drag each mound into a streak across the platter. Artfully arrange the salad down the middle of the platter. Top with the remaining chile rings and serve right away.

SERVES 8

I picked up some seeds for Padrón peppers on a trip to Spain and handed them over to Andy Griffin, who owns Mariquita Farm on California's central coast. I reap the benefits of my gift with this simple yet delicious dish. The heat can vary from pepper to pepper, so watch out for the hot ones.

CHARRED PADRÓN PEPPERS & CHERRY TOMATOES

¼ cup (2 fl oz/60 ml) extra-virgin olive oil

6 oz (185 g) Padrón peppers (about 50 peppers)

2 cups (12 oz/375 g) cherry tomatoes, in assorted colors, with stems intact

Sea salt, preferably Halen Môn (see Sources), and freshly ground black pepper

1 cup (1 oz/30 g) fresh opal basil leaves

¼ cup (2 fl oz/60 ml) Aioli (page 161)

Place a large sauté pan over medium-high heat. While the pan is heating, ready all of the ingredients, as this dish cooks quickly.

When the pan is very hot, add the olive oil and then throw in the peppers and tomatoes. (Be sure to leave the tomato stems intact so the tomatoes don't burst when they are charring in the pan.) Cook, shaking the pan occasionally to char all sides. The peppers and tomatoes will inflate at first; they are done when all sides are charred and they deflate, about 3 minutes. If your pan is not very large, work in batches to avoid crowding. Season with salt and then add the basil. Once the basil is added, remove the pan from the heat, season to taste with pepper, and pour onto a platter. Serve right away with the aioli for dipping.

SERVES 4

for the Aioli

crushed garlic

Dijon mustard

extra virgin olive oil

egg yolks

For this dish, I started with the classic clams in white wine sauce of my childhood and made it a bit more elegant. Crisp Prosecco and floral verbena combine to make a dish that will surprise everyone. Carry it covered to the table so that when you lift the lid, the fragrance of the sauce fills the air. I like to use a cataplana, a Portuguese pan shaped like two clamshells hinged at one end.

CLAMS, PROSECCO & LEMON VERBENA

1–2 tbsp semolina

36 small clams, preferably manila or savory, scrubbed

3 tbsp extra-virgin olive oil

⅔ cup (2½ oz/75 g) sliced shallots

⅓ cup (3 fl oz/80 ml) Prosecco

½ cup (4 fl oz/125 ml) Fish Stock (page 165)

1 cup (1 oz/30 g) fresh lemon verbena leaves

1 tbsp fresh lemon juice

Kosher salt

Fill a large bowl three-fourths full with salted water, add the semolina, and stir. Submerge the clams in the water and let stand for 30 minutes, agitating them occasionally to simulate an ocean tide and help them purge any sand. While the clams are soaking, ready all of the remaining ingredients, as this dish cooks quickly.

When the clams have finished soaking, lift them out of the water, transfer them to a colander, and rinse them under cold running water. (Do not pour the clams out of the bowl into the colander or you will pour the sand back over them.)

In a large cataplana or sauté pan with a lid, warm 2 tablespoons of the olive oil over medium heat. Add the shallots and sauté until translucent, 6–8 minutes. Pour in the Prosecco and stir gently. Add the clams and cook until the wine is reduced by half. Add the stock and lemon verbena, cover, and cook, shaking the pan occasionally, until nearly all of the clams have opened, about 3 minutes.

Add the remaining 1 tablespoon olive oil and the lemon juice to the pan and stir to mix. Taste the broth and adjust the seasoning with salt if needed. Bring the cataplana to the table, or divide the clams, broth, and lemon verbena evenly among warmed individual bowls, discarding any clams that failed to open, and serve right away. Use the lid of the opened cataplana, or put out an extra bowl, for your guests to fill with empty clam shells.

SERVES 4

When local albacore is in season in San Francisco, I can't get enough of it. Although albacore is in the tuna family, it needs to be cooked more than most other types of tuna, so I like to confit it and serve it as a cold salad. That also means that you can cook it when the weather is cool and pull it out and eat it on a hot day.

ALBACORE CONSERVA, FENNEL & OLIVES

ALBACORE CONSERVA

1-lb (500-g) piece albacore loin, trimmed of skin

Kosher salt and coarsely ground black pepper

1 tbsp coarsely ground fennel seeds

1 tbsp coarsely ground coriander seeds

1 tsp red pepper flakes

1 tsp sugar

2 or 3 fresh thyme sprigs

2 or 3 fresh flat-leaf parsley sprigs

2 or 3 fresh basil sprigs

3 bay leaves

4 cloves garlic, unpeeled, cracked

Zest of 1 lemon, in strips

1–1½ qt (32–48 fl oz/ 1–1.5 l) extra-virgin olive oil

2 fennel bulbs with fronds

Divide the albacore loin in half crosswise. Then, cut the thickest portion into 4 uniform logs, cutting once lengthwise and once crosswise, with each log about the same diameter as the tail half of the loin.

Season the albacore pieces evenly on all sides with 2 tablespoons salt, 1 tablespoon pepper, the fennel and coriander seeds, pepper flakes, and sugar. Arrange the pieces in a deep glass or ceramic baking dish in which they fit fairly snuggly and add the thyme, parsley, basil, bay, garlic, and lemon zest, distributing them evenly. Cover with plastic wrap and refrigerate for 4 hours.

Preheat the oven to 300°F (150°C).

Add olive oil to the baking dish to submerge the fish fully. Bake, checking occasionally to make sure the oil does not boil, until the fish is flaky but not dry when tested with a fork, about 30 minutes. At this point, the fish will be slightly underdone, but it will continue to cook as it sits. If the oil does begin to boil, reduce the heat slightly.

Remove the dish from the oven and let the albacore cool in the oil to room temperature before using. (The albacore may be stored submerged in the oil in an airtight container in the refrigerator for up to 1 week.)

Trim the stalks and fronds from the fennel bulbs. Discard the stalks and all but ¼ cup (¼ oz/7 g) of the fronds. Using a mandoline or other vegetable slicer, cut the fennel bulb lengthwise into paper-thin slices. Set the fronds aside for garnish. Then, cut the celery heart lengthwise into paper-thin slices. In a bowl, combine

1 celery heart, leaves reserved

¼ cup (¼ oz/7 g) salt-brined small black olives, preferably San Remo, pitted and cracked

¼ cup (¼ oz/7 g) fresh flat-leaf parsley leaves

About 2 tbsp Lemon Vinaigrette (page 160), or to your taste

the fennel and celery slices, olives, and parsley and toss to combine. Lightly dress the mixture, just to moisten the ingredients slightly, and toss gently.

Remove the albacore pieces from the oil. Using your fingers, flake the pieces into large chunks, dropping them into a second bowl. Drizzle with the vinaigrette, season with salt and pepper, and turn to coat evenly. Let stand for a few minutes.

To serve, divide the albacore evenly among individual plates, arranging it in a few piles. Then, arrange the fennel mixture over the top of the tuna and around the plate. Garnish with the fennel fronds and celery leaves and serve right away.

SERVES 6

top loin

bottom loin

belly area

two loin sections per fish: top loin and bottom loin

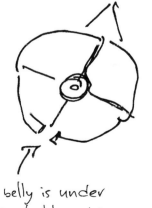

belly is under the bottom loin

cut one loin into logs for conserva

Foie gras and corn are made for each other: the richness of the liver pairs perfectly with the natural sweetness of the kernels. I paint each serving bowl with a swoosh of onion charcoal, which gives the raw corn kernels and the corn pudding a subtle grilled taste without the corn ever getting near the fire.

FOIE GRAS, CORN & ONION CHARCOAL

ONION CHARCOAL

6 bunches green onions (about 12 oz/375 g)

½ cup plus 3 tbsp (5½ fl oz/175 ml) extra-virgin olive oil

Kosher salt

7 ears corn, husks and silk removed

Kosher salt and freshly ground black pepper

1 lobe fresh foie gras, about 1¼ lb (625 g)

3 cipollini onions, sliced into rings about ¼ inch (6 mm) thick

1 tsp fresh tarragon leaves

1 tsp fresh lime juice

2 tbsp pesticide-free marigold petals

Preheat the oven to 500°F (260°C).

To make the onion charcoal, trim the green onions but leave them whole. Arrange the onions in a single layer on a rimmed baking sheet, place in the oven, and roast until black—yes, burn them—about 20 minutes.

Remove the onions from the oven and let cool completely. Transfer the cooled onions to a blender, add the olive oil and ¼ teaspoon salt, and process until smooth, about 5 minutes. Use immediately, or transfer to a container with a tight-fitting lid and refrigerate for up to 2 months.

Reduce the oven heat to 450°F (230°C).

Cut the kernels from the corncobs, and reserve the cobs. Set aside 1 cup (6 oz/185 g) of the corn kernels. Run the back of a knife blade along the length of each corncob to force out any juice and the germ of each kernel into a bowl. Transfer the remaining corn kernels and the corncob scrapings to a blender and process until smooth. Strain through a fine-mesh sieve into a small saucepan, pressing firmly on the solids with the back of a ladle. You should have about 2 cups (16 fl oz/500 ml). Place over medium heat and bring to a simmer, stirring constantly with a heatproof silicone spatula until the mixture is thickened to a puddinglike consistency, about 2 minutes. Remove from the heat, season with salt, and cover to keep warm.

Rinse the foie gras under running cool water and pat dry with paper towels. Trim away any blood and green spots. Using a small

Cut kernels
off the cob

sharp knife, score the foie gras on the smooth, top side with cross-hatching, cutting just barely into the liver, and then season with salt and pepper. Let stand for about 10 minutes.

Meanwhile, place a large sauté pan over high heat. Add the onion rings in a single layer and cook, turning once, until nicely charred on both sides, 4–8 minutes on each side. Transfer to a plate.

Place an ovenproof sauté pan over high heat. When hot, place the foie gras, scored side down, in the pan and sear until golden brown, about 2 minutes. Flip the foie gras over and transfer to the oven. Roast until soft to the touch and hot throughout, about 5 minutes. Transfer to a cutting board.

Have ready 6 shallow bowls. Toss the tarragon with the lime juice. Using a wide, clean paint-brush, and using about 1 teaspoon per bowl, paint a streak of the onion charcoal in each bowl up to the rim. Divide the corn pudding among the bowls. Cut the foie gras into 6 equal portions and place a portion in each bowl. Top each with the reserved corn kernels, onion rings, and tarragon. Sprinkle with the marigold petals and serve right away.

SERVES 6

These kernels have been cut
too deep, leaving bitter, woody
cob pieces on the ends

Perfectly cut kernels:
not too deep,
look like teeth

Mixing the components of a classic puttanesca sauce with diced raw rib eye, and topping the mixture with deep-fried garlic chips, produces a spicy new take on traditional beef tartare. Do not discard the oil used for frying the garlic chips. Store it in an airtight container in a cool place and use in vinaigrettes or for marinating meats.

BEEF TARTARE PUTTANESCA

2 lb (1 kg) grass-fed beef rib eye

15 small cherry tomatoes

2 serrano chiles, sliced into paper-thin rings

2 tbsp finely diced red onion

2 tbsp chopped small salt-brined black olives, preferably San Remo

2 tbsp minced marinated white anchovies

2 tsp salted small capers, well rinsed

1 tsp finely grated lemon zest

Extra-virgin olive oil

1 tbsp red wine vinegar

4 tsp *each* finely sliced fresh basil leaves and mint leaves

Sea salt, preferably Halen Môn (see Sources), and coarsely ground black pepper

Garlic Chips (page 163)

Grilled or toasted baguette slices

Chill 1 large bowl and 8 individual plates.

Trim the beef of any sinew or gristle. Cut the beef into ¼-inch (6-mm) dice. As the beef is cut, place the pieces in the chilled bowl. Halve the tomatoes through the stem end and add them to the bowl with the beef. Add the chiles, onion, olives, anchovies, capers, and lemon zest and mix gently, being careful not to break up the tomatoes. Add a splash of olive oil, the vinegar, basil, and mint and mix well. Season with salt and pepper, then taste and adjust the seasoning. You are looking for a nice balance of meat to other ingredients and a good amount of spice.

To serve, divide the meat mixture evenly among the chilled plates, mounding it slightly to make an attractive presentation. Drizzle each serving with a little olive oil and then sprinkle with the garlic chips. Serve with the baguette slices.

SERVES 8

The first time I smelled a pot of tripe simmering on the stove, I ran the other direction. That's when I was a kid. Now, I run straight for it. This is a great salad for a hot day. Both the lemony dressing with a hint of chile and the creamy potato slices tamp down the richness of the tripe.

MARINATED TRIPE, NEW POTATOES & PARSLEY

1⅓ cups (5½ oz/170 g) *each* coarsely chopped carrot, celery, and onion

2 heads garlic, split, plus 5 cloves, minced

1 bunch fresh thyme

2 bay leaves

1 tbsp fennel seeds

Kosher salt

2 vanilla beans, split lengthwise

½ cup (4 fl oz/125 ml) dry white wine

Juice of 1 lemon

4 tbsp (2 fl oz/60 ml) Champagne vinegar

2 lb (1 kg) honeycomb beef tripe, preferably organic and unbleached

10 fingerling potatoes

1 tbsp red pepper flakes

Finely grated zest and juice of 3 Bearss limes or Eureka lemons

½ cup (4 fl oz/125 ml) extra-virgin olive oil, plus more for drizzling

3 tbsp coarsely chopped fresh flat-leaf parsley

In a large stockpot, combine 8 cups (8 l) water, the carrot, celery, onion, split garlic heads, thyme, bay, fennel seeds, 1 tablespoon salt, the vanilla, wine, lemon juice, and 1 tablespoon of the vinegar. Rinse the tripe well under cold running water until the water runs clear and the tripe is free of grit. Add the tripe to the pot, place over medium-high heat, and bring to a boil. Reduce the heat so that the liquid just simmers and cook uncovered, skimming any scum that rises to the surface, until the tripe is very tender, about 3 hours. Remove from the heat, let the tripe cool completely in the cooking liquid, and refrigerate the tripe in the liquid overnight.

Place the potatoes in a large saucepan with salted water to cover, bring to a simmer, and cook until just tender when pierced with a knife, 10–15 minutes. Drain, rinse under cold running water to cool completely, and then cut crosswise into slices ¼ inch (6 mm) thick. Place in a bowl. Remove the tripe from the cooking liquid and discard the liquid. Using a very sharp knife, shave the tripe into thin, ribbonlike strips. Transfer to a bowl. In a small bowl, combine the minced garlic, pepper flakes, lime zest and juice, and remaining 3 tablespoons vinegar and let stand for 5 minutes. Slowly whisk in the olive oil and season with salt. Add just enough of the vinaigrette to the tripe to coat lightly and then toss to mix. Taste and add more vinaigrette to your liking. Add the remaining vinaigrette to the potatoes and toss gently to coat evenly. Add the potatoes to the tripe and toss together.

Transfer the tripe and potatoes to a platter and garnish with parsley and a drizzle of olive oil. Serve right away.

SERVES 6

I created this in honor of New York chef David Chang, who famously once said, "Every restaurant in San Francisco is just serving figs on a plate." Not surprisingly, that remark pissed off a lot of people in the city. But I was glad he said it, because it created a dialogue for change. Thanks, David, for stirring the pot!

FIGS, MARCONA ALMONDS & PORT VINAIGRETTE

12 figs

1 cup (1 oz/30 g) arugula, preferably wild

¼ cup (1 oz/30 g) finely julienned red onion

½ cup (2½ oz/75 g) roasted, salted Marcona almonds

Sea salt, preferably Halen Môn (see Sources), and freshly ground black pepper

2 tbsp Port Vinaigrette (page 161)

Cut any tough stems off of the figs. Quarter the figs lengthwise and place in a single layer, cut side up, on a large plate. In a bowl, combine the arugula, onion, and almonds and season with salt and pepper. Drizzle with 1 tablespoon of the vinaigrette and toss to coat lightly and evenly.

Season the figs with salt, pepper, and the remaining 1 tablespoon vinaigrette. Scatter the salad over the top of the figs. Serve right away.

SERVES 4

fall

Sometimes, the best way to start a meal is with a drink. But this is more than a drink—it's like a first course all by itself! The combination of beer, tomatoes, and oysters, bolstered with chiles and fish sauce, has proven an excellent hangover cure.

BLOODY ROMAN

1 tbsp salt-packed capers

2 red Fresno chiles

3 lb (1.5 kg) heirloom tomatoes

1 shallot, finely diced

2 tbsp chopped pickled peppers, preferably Mama Lil's brand (see Sources)

2 tsp Asian fish sauce, preferably Red Boat brand #50 (see Sources)

1 tsp Cabernet vinegar

1 tsp ground Aleppo pepper

Kosher salt and freshly ground black pepper

1 tbsp chopped fresh flat-leaf parsley

18 Castelvetrano or other mild green olives, pitted

3 bottles (12 fl oz/375 ml each) beer, preferably Anchor Steam, cold

12 oysters, preferably Kumamato or Kusshi, shucked, liquor reserved

6 serrano chiles

Chile threads (see Sources)

Chill six 1-pint (16–fl oz/500-ml) glasses in the refrigerator.

To make the Roman mix, rinse and chop the capers. Seed and chop the chiles. Core and coarsely chop the tomatoes, then pass the tomatoes through a food mill fitted with the fine grinding disk placed over a bowl to remove the skins and seeds. Add the shallot, capers, and chiles to the bowl with the tomatoes and mix well. Season with the pickled peppers, fish sauce, vinegar, and Aleppo pepper and mix well. Season to taste with salt and pepper and stir in the parsley.

Place 2 pitted olives in each chilled glass. Divide the beer evenly among the glasses, and then top off each glass with the Roman mix. Place 2 shucked oysters and their liquor in each glass and then garnish each serving with an olive, serrano chile, and chile threads. Serve right away.

SERVES 6

Every year, my business partner's in-laws bring us persimmons from their backyard. One year they had a bumper crop and this salad was born out of trying to come up with ways to use the fruits before they spoiled. Using nocino, the green walnut liqueur from Emilia-Romagna, enhances the flavor of the walnuts.

PERSIMMON, BLACK WALNUTS, WATERCRESS & NOCINO

NOCINO VINAIGRETTE

3 cups (24 fl oz/750 l) *nocino* liqueur

1 tbsp sherry vinegar

Dash of fresh lemon juice

Kosher salt and freshly ground black pepper

¼ cup (2 fl oz/60 ml) extra-virgin olive oil

¼ cup (1 oz/30 g) black walnuts

1 tbsp extra-virgin olive oil

Kosher salt and freshly ground black pepper

3 Fuyu persimmons

2 bunches watercress, tough stems removed

To make the vinaigrette, pour the *nocino* into a nonreactive saucepan, place over low heat, and simmer until reduced to 1 cup (8 fl oz/250 ml), 15–20 minutes (the liqueur is flammable, so watch it closely while it is reducing and be sure to keep it over low heat.) Transfer the liqueur to a bowl and let cool to room temperature. Once the liqueur is cool, whisk in the vinegar, lemon juice, a pinch of salt, and a few grinds of pepper and then slowly whisk in the ¼ cup (2 fl oz/60 ml) olive oil until emulsified. You should have about 2½ cups (20 fl oz/625 ml). You will need only about 2 tablespoons for this recipe. Cover and refrigerate the remainder for another use. It will keep for up to 4 days.

Preheat the oven to 350°F (180°C). In a small bowl, toss the walnuts with the 1 tablespoon olive oil, season with salt and pepper, and then spread in a small, shallow pan. Place in the oven and toast until aromatic, about 5 minutes. Let cool completely.

Peel the persimmons. Using a mandoline or other vegetable slicer, cut each persimmon into paper-thin slices, being careful to avoid the seeds. In a bowl, combine the watercress and persimmons. Crush the toasted walnuts in your hands and add to the bowl. Season the salad with salt and pepper and then dress lightly with the vinaigrette.

To serve, divide the salad evenly among individual plates and grind a little pepper over each salad. Serve right away.

SERVES 4

The smell of fresh figs roasting on their own leaves is intoxicating. The leaves give off an almost coconut-like aroma, and caramelized ricotta adds richness to the sweet fruit. You can double or triple this for larger groups, but the best thing about it is that it can be served either as a beginning or an ending.

ROASTED FIGS, SHEEP'S MILK RICOTTA & FIG LEAVES

2 large fig leaves
(see Sources)

6 ripe fresh figs, preferably
2 or 3 different varieties

2 tbsp extra-virgin olive oil

Sea salt, preferably Halen Môn (see Sources), and freshly ground black pepper

6 tbsp (3 oz/90 g) sheep's milk ricotta cheese

Preheat the oven to 450°F (230°C).

Remove the thick stem at the base of each fig leaf. Cut any tough stems off of the figs. Place the fig leaves, stem end to stem end, in a broiler-safe roasting pan just large enough to accommodate them. Drizzle 1 tablespoon of the olive oil evenly on the leaves and season lightly with salt and pepper. Place the figs, standing them upright and clustered together, on the leaves. Then, using a sharp knife, cut an X in the top of each fig, cutting halfway down the height of the fig. Gently squeeze each fig at its base so the X opens and the fig looks like it is blooming. Place 1 tablespoon of the ricotta in the center of each "bloom." Season the ricotta lightly with salt and pepper and drizzle with the remaining 1 tablespoon olive oil.

Place in the oven and roast for 12 minutes. The figs and cheese should meld together but the figs should not be falling apart. Turn the oven setting to broil, move the dish a few inches from the heat source, and broil until the tops blister, about 1 minute.

Using a large, wide spatula, transfer the figs and the leaves to a serving platter and serve right away.

SERVES 2

The flavors of this simple combination of sweet, creamy pumpkin, tart pickled cranberries, and bitter mustard greens are the essence of fall. To intensify the pumpkin flavor, I use toasted seeds and pumpkin seed oil. This dish would be a great first course for Thanksgiving or a good accompaniment to roasted game birds.

PUMPKIN, PUMPKIN SEEDS & PICKLED CRANBERRIES

PICKLED CRANBERRIES

1 lb (500 g) cranberries

2 tbsp yellow mustard seeds

Kosher salt

2 cups (16 fl oz/500 ml) cider vinegar

2 cups (14 oz/440 g) firmly packed brown sugar

1 bay leaf

1 fresh sage sprig

2 fresh thyme sprigs

1 tsp coriander seeds

1 tsp fennel seeds

1 tsp black peppercorns

1 Sugar Pie pumpkin, about 1.5 lb (750 g)

2 tbsp rendered duck fat

⅓ cup (1½ oz/45 g) pumpkin seeds

¼ cup (¼ oz/7 g) fresh sage leaves

2 cups (2 oz/60 g) baby red mustard greens

Pumpkin seed oil for drizzling

To make the pickled cranberries, place the berries in a nonreactive container with the mustard seeds and a pinch of salt. In a saucepan, bring the vinegar, sugar, bay, sage, thyme, coriander and fennel seeds, and peppercorns to a boil over high heat. Remove from the heat, then pour the hot liquid through a fine-mesh sieve over the cranberries. Discard the solids in the sieve. Place a pot lid on top of the cranberries, then place a large, sealed plastic container filled with water on top to keep the berries submerged. Let the cranberries stand in the liquid until cool.

Meanwhile, halve, seed, and peel the pumpkin, then cut it into 1-inch (2.5-cm) cubes. Bring a large saucepan three-fourths full of salted water to a boil over high heat. Add the pumpkin cubes and cook until tender, 3–4 minutes. Drain well and spread the pumpkin cubes on a rimmed baking sheet. Let cool completely.

In a large sauté pan over high heat, warm the duck fat. When hot, add the pumpkin cubes and cook, tossing occasionally, until caramelized, about 4 minutes. Add the pumpkin seeds and sage and sauté until toasted, about 2 minutes. Fold in the mustard greens and cook briefly just until wilted and warm.

To serve, remove the plastic container and lid and warm the cranberries in their pickling liquid over low heat until warmed through. Divide the pumpkin-mustard greens mixture among warmed individual bowls and drizzle each serving with pumpkin seed oil. Use a slotted spoon to divide the cranberries among the bowls (discard the pickling liquid) and serve right away.

SERVES 4

This recipe calls for Medjool dates, which are big, meaty, chewy, and moist. They are also quite sweet, a quality that is nicely balanced by combining them with salty capers and anchovies and toasted nuts. This dish is great alongside roasted or grilled lamb.

DATES, CAPERS & ANCHOVIES

16 Medjool dates

3 tbsp extra-virgin olive oil

2 tbsp pine nuts

¼ cup (¼ oz/7 g) fresh mint leaves

2 tbsp salted small capers, well rinsed

12 marinated white anchovy fillets

Kosher salt

Make a small lengthwise incision in each date and remove the pit, making sure to keep the dates whole.

This dish cooks quickly, so have all of your ingredients ready before you begin to cook. In a large sauté pan over high heat, combine the olive oil and dates. When the dates begin to blister, after about 1 minute, add the pine nuts and mint. Both the mint and the nuts will toast quickly. As soon as they do, add the capers and anchovies and season with a pinch of salt.

Divide evenly among individual plates or transfer to a serving platter. Serve right away.

SERVES 4

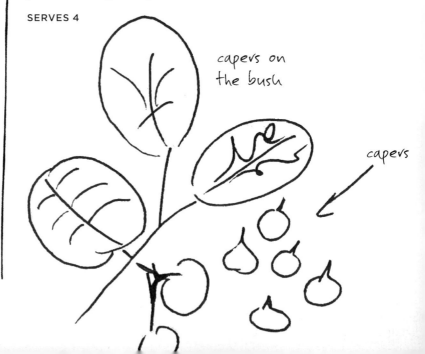

capers on the bush

capers

Mark Miller, my first chef out of culinary school, always said to me, "More acid! More herbs!" This recipe is a perfect example of that advice, with lots of vinegar and fresh herbs in the pickling liquid to enhance the earthiness of the mushrooms. Nepitella is known as wild Tuscan mint and is always paired with mushrooms.

PICKLED MUSHROOM & RICOTTA BRUSCHETTA

PICKLED MUSHROOMS

7 tbsp (3½ fl oz/105 ml) Champagne vinegar

1 cup (8 fl oz/250 ml) dry white wine

2 fresh *nepitella* or mint sprigs

1 Douglas fir sprig, about 6 inches (15 cm) long

1 juniper berry, cracked

4 shallots, sliced into rings

1 red Fresno chile, sliced into rings

1 head garlic, split crosswise

Kosher salt and freshly ground black pepper

1 lb (500 g) assorted wild or cultivated mushrooms such as chanterelle, candy cap, maitake, and baby shiitake, brushed clean and trimmed

1 cup (8 fl oz/250 ml) extra-virgin olive oil, or more if needed

To make the pickled mushrooms, in a saucepan, combine 1 cup (8 fl oz/250 ml) water, the vinegar, and wine and bring a boil over high heat. Add the *nepitella*, Douglas fir, juniper, shallots, chile, garlic, and 1 tablespoon salt and then finally add the mushrooms. Bring the liquid back to a boil, then turn off the heat.

Drain the mushrooms into a sieve and transfer them to a bowl along with the other solid ingredients. Taste and adjust the seasonings with salt and pepper. While still warm, pour enough olive oil over the mushrooms to cover. Cover and refrigerate the mushrooms overnight, or up to 3 weeks before using.

Bring the mushrooms to room temperature. Prepare a medium-hot fire in a charcoal or gas grill or preheat a stove-top grill pan over medium-high heat.

Brush both sides of each bread slice with olive oil and then season both sides with salt and pepper. Place the bread slices on the grill rack and let cook undisturbed until crisp, but not burnt, and brown grill marks are starting to form. The timing will depend upon the bread you use and the heat of your grill—pick up an edge using tongs and take a peek to check for doneness. Using the tongs, rotate each slice 90 degrees and leave undisturbed for several seconds (take another peek to check) to create uniform cross-hatching on the underside. Using the tongs, turn the slices over and repeat to crosshatch the second side the same way. Be sure the bread is evenly grilled and not overcooked.

4 large slices coarse country bread, 1 inch (2.5 cm) thick

Extra-virgin olive oil for brushing

Kosher salt and freshly ground black pepper

1 cup (8 oz/250 g) sheep's milk ricotta

1½ cups (1½ oz/45 g) mâche

Spread each slice of bread with one-fourth of the ricotta. Using a slotted spoon, divide the mushrooms evenly among the bread slices, arranging them on top of the cheese. Cut each bread slice in half on an angle and place the halves on a plate. Top each bruschetta with one-fourth of the mâche and season with pepper. Serve right away.

SERVES 4

Douglas fir young tips only

This is based on a dish that my business partner, Mark Pastore, described to me from memory. The key to its success is a flavorful dandelion braising liquid, because it is all about the bread soaking up the broth. The chiles and the pecorino add just the right amount of sweet heat and sharpness.

BRAISED DANDELION GREENS, CHILE & PECORINO

2 tbsp olive oil

1 yellow onion, finely diced (about 1 cup/5 oz/155 g)

1 head garlic, split crosswise

5 dried chiles such as guajillo or ancho, seeded

1 lb (500 g) dandelion greens, tough stems removed, leaves cut crosswise into wide strips

5½ cups (44 fl oz/1.35 l) Chicken Stock (page 164)

4-inch (10-cm) piece pecorino cheese rind

Kosher salt and freshly ground black pepper

3 tbsp fruity extra-virgin olive oil, preferably Coratina brand (see Sources), plus more for drizzling

6 baguette slices

1 lemon

Wedge of pecorino cheese for shaving

In a large pot over medium heat, warm the 2 tablespoons olive oil. Add the onion and garlic and cook, stirring occasionally, until the onion is translucent, about 5 minutes. Add the chiles and continue to cook, stirring, until lightly toasted, about 5 minutes more.

Add the dandelion greens and toss and stir occasionally until wilted. Add the stock and pecorino rind, bring to a simmer, and cook until tender, 20–30 minutes. (Bigger greens will take longer to cook.) Season with salt and pepper and then stir in the 3 tablespoons extra-virgin olive oil to balance the bitterness of the greens.

While the dandelion greens are cooking, prepare a medium fire in a charcoal or gas grill or preheat a stove-top grill pan over medium-high heat. Grill the baguette slices, turning once, until etched with grill marks on both sides and crisp, about 2 minutes on each side. Remove from the heat and rub one side of each slice with the whole lemon, releasing the natural oils of the zest to flavor the bread.

To serve, place each baguette slice in an individual bowl. Place the dandelion greens over the bread, dividing evenly, and then ladle the liquid over the top (the liquid is the best part). Using a vegetable peeler, shave a few pecorino curls over the top and then drizzle with a little extra-virgin olive oil. Grind a little pepper over each bowl and serve right away.

SERVES 6

I first made this salad many years ago for a demo at the farmers' market. It was a way to make fun of some of the shoppers who were complaining that the vegetables were dirty when they bought them. What could be better than earthy root vegetables paired with the earthiness of fresh truffle?

DIRTY VEGETABLES

CHAMPAGNE VINAIGRETTE

2 tbsp Champagne vinegar

1 tsp fresh lemon juice

2 tbsp pure olive oil

2 tbsp extra-virgin olive oil

Kosher salt and freshly ground black pepper

2 baby Chioggia beets, peeled

2 baby golden beets, peeled

1 yellow carrot, peeled

1 red carrot, peeled

1 orange carrot, peeled

2 baby turnips, peeled

Kosher salt and freshly ground black pepper

2 cups (2 oz/60 g) mâche

1 fresh black truffle

To make the vinaigrette, in a small bowl, whisk together the vinegar, lemon juice, and olive oils until emulsified. Season to taste with salt and pepper and set aside.

Using a mandoline or other vegetable slicer, slice the beets, carrots, and turnips paper-thin, cutting each of them into a different shape that showcases their color and vibrancy. Place all of the vegetable slices in a bowl and season with salt and pepper. Drizzle with the vinaigrette and toss to coat evenly. Arrange the vegetable slices on a platter and top with the mâche. Using a Microplane or other fine-rasp grater, grate the truffle over the top of the dish—this is the "dirt." Serve right away.

SERVES 4

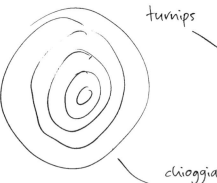

carrots

All cut paper-thin on a mandoline

turnips

chioggia beets

Cooking food in parchment is a classic technique in which foods enclosed in a paper package cook quickly in a moist, aromatic cloud of steam. As the ingredients cook, the juice from the porcini and the melted foie gras fat combine to create an amazing jus. Be sure to snip open the package at the table so your guests can breathe in the intoxicating aroma.

PORCINI, FOIE GRAS & DOUGLAS FIR

3 porcini mushrooms,
2 oz (60 g) each

3 Douglas fir sprigs,
each about 6 inches
(15 cm) long

6-oz (185-g) piece fresh
foie gras

Kosher salt and freshly
ground black pepper

Preheat the oven to 450°F (230°C).

Trim the base of the stem of each mushroom and then scrape the stems to remove any dirt. Wipe the caps clean with a damp paper towel and quarter the mushrooms through the stem end.

Fold an 18-inch (45-cm) long sheet of parchment paper in half crosswise. Unfold the sheet and place the fir sprigs on the bottom, near the fold. Lay the mushroom quarters on top of the fir sprigs.

Rinse the foie gras under cool running water and pat dry with paper towels. Trim away any blood and green spots. Using a small sharp knife, score the foie gras on the larger 2 sides with cross-hatching, cutting just barely into the liver, and then season with salt and pepper. Season the mushrooms with salt and pepper and place the foie gras on top of the mushrooms.

Fold over the parchment paper to cover the contents. Then, starting at one corner, turn the edges of the parchment over to make a small fold. Continue to make small, overlapping folds around the entire edge of the parchment package, sealing it securely closed.

Place the parchment package in a 12-inch (30-cm) ovenproof sauté pan, place the pan over medium heat, and cook until the parchment begins to puff, about 1 minute. Immediately place the pan in the oven and cook the package for 12 minutes. Listen to hear the sizzle inside the parchment.

Remove the pan from the oven and, using two metal spatulas, immediately transfer the package to a platter before the parchment collapses. Bring the platter to the table right away, and, using scissors, snip open the package, cutting down the center. Carefully open the packet and serve the foie gras and mushrooms right away.

SERVES 4

Put ingredients in the center of the bottom half of the parchment

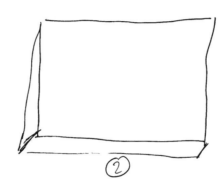

Fold the parchment over to cover

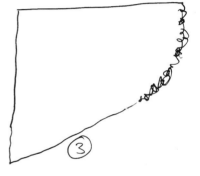

Starting at the corner, fold the edges in a small section at a time

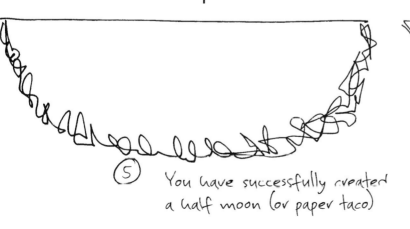

You have successfully created a half moon (or paper taco)

Continue folding to seal the package

Now look at the finished dish on the next page because I didn't want to draw it!

In the wine country north of San Francisco, growers are crushing their grapes this time of year. That's when I put this salad on the menu. I use a mix of table and wine grapes for a range of tart and sweet flavors.

PAN-ROASTED GRAPES, TURNIPS & GRAPE LEAVES

4 sprigs fresh tarragon

Pure olive oil for sautéing and shallow frying

1 cup (6 oz/190 g) Red Flame seedless grapes

1 cup (6 oz/190 g) Thompson seedless grapes

1 cup (6 oz/190 g) muscat grapes

1 cup (6 oz/190 g) Nebbiolo or Concord grapes

12 young grape leaves

Kosher salt and freshly ground black pepper

6 baby turnips with tops

2 tbsp Brovada (page 162)

Pick the leaves from the tarragon sprigs. Reserve the stems.

In a sauté pan over high heat, warm 2 tablespoons olive oil. When it is hot, add all of the grapes and tarragon stems and cook, shaking the pan to heat the grapes evenly, until the grapes are blistered, about 3 minutes. Be careful not to overcook the grapes or they will turn to mush. Transfer the grapes to a rimmed baking sheet, spreading them in a single layer, and let cool completely. Discard the tarragon stems.

Line a baking sheet with paper towels. Pour olive oil to a depth of ¼ inch (6 mm) into a deep sauté pan and heat to 350°F (180°C) on a deep-frying thermometer. Add the grape leaves and fry until crisp, about 10 seconds. Using tongs, transfer to the towel-lined baking sheet and season with salt and pepper.

When the grapes are cool, transfer them to a bowl and add the tarragon leaves. Using a mandoline or other vegetable slicer, cut the turnips, including a bit of the green at the top, into paper-thin slices. Add the turnips to the grapes. Drizzle with the *brovada* and toss to coat evenly.

To serve, put the grape mixture on a platter or divide it evenly among individual plates. Crumble the grape leaves with your hands and scatter evenly over the top. Sprinkle the top with pepper and serve right away.

SERVES 4

I love the flavor and crisp acidity of apples, and when they are in season, I eat them all the time out of hand. I also like to use them in the kitchen. In this dish, I combine them with dandelion greens, which provide a nice bitter note, and hazelnuts, which lend richness and crunch to the dish.

APPLE, DANDELION & HAZELNUTS

APPLE CIDER VINAIGRETTE

½ cup (4 fl oz/125 ml) apple cider

¼ cup (2 fl oz/60 ml) cider vinegar

Kosher salt and freshly ground black pepper

¼ tsp ground Aleppo pepper

¾ cup (6 fl oz/180 ml) extra-virgin olive oil

½ cup (2½ oz/75 g) hazelnuts

1 tbsp extra-virgin olive oil

Kosher salt and freshly ground black pepper

3 apples, in different varieties, such as Macintosh, Gravenstein, or Mutsu

¼ lb (125 g) baby dandelion greens

¼ cup (¼ oz/7 g) fresh chive batons (1-inch/ 2.5-cm lengths)

¼ cup (¾ oz/20 g) dandelion flowers or marigold petals

Preheat the oven to 325°F (165°C).

To make the vinaigrette, in a small bowl, whisk together the apple cider, vinegar, a pinch each of salt and pepper, and the Aleppo pepper. Drizzle in the olive oil, whisking constantly until emulsified. Taste and adjust the seasoning if needed and set aside.

In a small bowl, toss the nuts with the 1 tablespoon olive oil and a little salt and pepper, coating them evenly. Spread the nuts in a single layer on a small rimmed baking sheet or metal pie pan and toast until golden brown, about 10 minutes. Let cool completely, then, using the bottom of a sturdy coffee mug, crack the nuts into large pieces.

Using a mandoline or other vegetable slicer, slice the apples paper-thin.

In a bowl, combine the apples, dandelion greens, and toasted hazelnuts, drizzle with some of the vinaigrette, and toss to coat evenly. Add the chives and flowers, toss to combine, and immediately divide among individual plates. Grind a little pepper over the top of each salad and serve right away.

SERVES 6

Ancient spice was found in the book of Apicius, a Roman cookery book that dates from the late fourth century. In those days, spices were used to mask the flavor of rancid meat. In this dish, the rub helps accentuate the natural flavor of the squab.

ROASTED SQUAB, ANCIENT SPICE & PICKLED GRAPES

PICKLED GRAPES

3 cups (24 fl oz/750 ml) red wine vinegar

½ cup (4 oz/125 g) sugar

Kosher salt

1 tbsp black peppercorns

1 tbsp fennel seeds

2 tsp yellow mustard seeds

1½ cups (9 oz/280 g) Red Flame seedless grapes

ANCIENT SPICE RUB

2 tbsp ground Aleppo pepper

2 tbsp whole cloves

2 tbsp juniper berries

2 tbsp allspice berries

2 tbsp cinnamon stick pieces

½ cup (2 oz/60 g) long pepper (see Sources)

(continued)

To prepare the pickled grapes, in a saucepan, combine the vinegar, sugar, 2 tablespoons salt, the peppercorns, fennel seeds, and mustard seeds and whisk together so the sugar and salt won't sink to the bottom. Bring to a boil over high heat, stirring to dissolve the sugar, and immediately remove from the heat. Let cool completely, transfer to a covered container, and refrigerate until well chilled.

Place the grapes in a bowl, pour the chilled liquid over the grapes, cover, and refrigerate for 24 hours.

To make the spice rub, in a spice grinder, combine the Aleppo pepper, cloves, juniper, allspice, cinnamon, and long pepper and grind to a powder. (Depending on the size of your grinder, you may need to do this in batches.)

To prepare the squabs, start by separating the legs from the body: Using a knife, cut in from the point of the breast following the curve of the frame, cutting through the spine so that the two legs from each bird are attached to each other. If the feet are still attached, be sure to cut the talons off the feet with a pair of scissors. Remove the wing tips. You should end up with four large pieces of squab, two leg-thigh portions and two breast-wing portions. Rub the spice rub evenly over the squab pieces. Place them on a plate and refrigerate, uncovered, for at least 4 hours or preferably overnight. (Leaving the pieces uncovered dries out the skin, which makes it easier to cook them crisp and golden brown.) (continued)

2 squabs

¼ cup (2 oz/60 g)
rendered duck fat

2 cups (2 oz/60 g)
pepper cress

Extra-virgin olive oil

Kosher salt and freshly
ground black pepper

Preheat the oven to 350°F (180°C). Remove the squab pieces from the refrigerator and let stand at room temperature for 15 minutes.

In an ovenproof sauté pan over medium heat, warm the duck fat. When hot, add the squab leg-thigh portions, skin side down, and sear, basting the top with the fat in the pan to help them cook through, until golden brown on the underside, about 4 minutes. Flip the pieces over and add the breast pieces, skin side down. Keeping the heat at medium to avoid burning the skin, cook the breast pieces, basting with the fat in the pan, until they are golden brown on the underside, about 5 minutes. Turn the breast pieces skin side up, transfer to the oven, and roast until the meat is firm to the touch and the joints move easily, about 6 minutes. Remove from the oven and let rest for 5 minutes before serving.

While the squabs are resting, drain the grapes and discard the pickling liquid. Split the grapes in half lengthwise, transfer to a bowl, and add the pepper cress.

To serve, arrange the squab on a platter. If desired, using a cleaver, split each portion in half lengthwise through the backbone. Drizzle the grapes and pepper cress lightly with olive oil, season with salt and pepper, and toss to coat evenly. Scatter the grapes and cress over the squabs and serve right away.

SERVES 4

How the squabs
should look
after separating

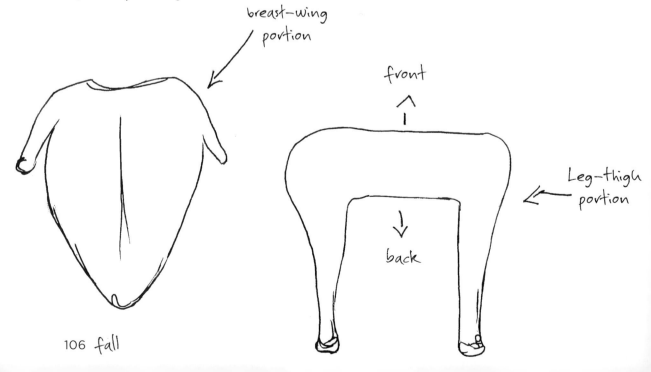

breast–wing
portion

front

Leg–thigh
portion

back

Meatballs are a staple in every house and in almost every culture. I love meatballs in a rich broth topped with freshly grated cheese. It is the perfect cure-all dish and a must have for when the sun starts going down earlier and the nights become crisp.

PORK & PORCINI POLPETTINI

1 tbsp extra-virgin olive oil

½ cup (2½ oz/75 g) *each* finely diced white onion, carrot, and celery

3 cloves garlic, minced

1 tbsp fresh thyme leaves

1 bay leaf

½ lb (250 g) fresh porcini mushrooms or stemmed shiitakes, brushed clean, stem ends trimmed, and finely diced

2 tbsp dry white wine

1 lb (500 g) ground pork

Kosher salt and freshly ground black pepper

2 large eggs, lightly beaten

2 cups (4 oz/125 g) finely diced day-old foccacia

8 cups (64 fl oz/2 l) Porcini Brodo (page 164)

¼ cup (¼ oz/7 g) *each* fresh flat-leaf parsley leaves and celery leaves

Wedge of Parmigiano-Reggiano cheese

In a sauté pan over medium heat, warm the olive oil. Add the onion, carrot, celery, garlic, thyme, and bay and sauté until the onion is translucent, about 8 minutes. Add the mushrooms and sauté for 3 minutes more. Add the wine and scrape any browned bits from the pan bottom. Cook until the wine evaporates and remove from the heat. Let cool completely.

Spread the ground pork in a flat, even layer in a large rimmed baking sheet. Season with salt and pepper, pour over the eggs and distribute the foccacia evenly over the top. Remove the bay leaf from the cooled vegetable mixture, then spread the mixture evenly over the pork. Now, working the ingredients as little as possible, bring all of the ingredients together into a uniform mixture (the more you work the meat, the tougher the meatballs will be). Sauté a nugget of the mixture, taste, and then adjust the seasoning of the mixture with salt and pepper. Using a 1-ounce ice cream scoop, quickly shape the mixture into small balls and place on a plate or baking sheet.

In a wide saucepan over medium heat, bring the porcini brodo to a gentle simmer. Carefully lower the meatballs into the broth, submerging them, and adjust the heat so that very few bubbles break on the surface. Cover the pan and cook until the meatballs are no longer pink in the center, 15–20 minutes.

To serve, stir the parsley and celery leaves into the pan with the meatballs. Divide the meatballs and broth among individual bowls. Grate Parmigiano-Reggiano cheese over the top.

SERVES 6

Quail is a little bird with a lot of flavor. I like to french the legs, which end up looking both out of place and oddly correct at the same time. The scent of rose geranium, when combined with apples and browned butter, evokes all the flavors and aromas of fall.

QUAIL, APPLES & ROSE GERANIUM

4 semi-boneless quail

3 tbsp unsalted butter

2 tart eating apples, such as Gravenstein or Mutsu

½ cup (½ oz/15 g) pesticide-free rose geranium leaves, plus petals for garnish

3 tbsp cider vinegar

Remove the wings and then remove the thigh bones from each quail but leave the drumsticks intact (the breastbones should already be removed). Trim around the base of each drumstick to remove the meat (this is called "frenching"). Repeat with the remaining quail. Place a quail on a work surface and cover with a zip-lock freezer bag. Using a meat mallet, pound the bird flat. You don't need to kill it—it is already dead—you just want it uniformly flattened so it cooks evenly. Repeat with the remaining birds.

In a large sauté pan over high heat, melt the butter. When the butter begins to brown, add the birds, breast side down, and cook, turning once, until browned on both sides and firm to the touch, about 4 minutes on each side. The meat will still be pink on the inside.

While the quail are cooking, halve and core the apples, but do not peel. Cut them into julienne and set aside.

Transfer the quail to individual plates or a platter and arrange the apples on top. Add the geranium leaves to the browned butter remaining in the pan and cook, turning as needed, until browned and crisp, about 10 seconds. Pour in the vinegar and scrape the browned bits from the pan bottom, and then pour the contents of the pan over the quail and apples. Garnish with the geranium petals and serve right away.

SERVES 4

winter

Beginning with bitter flavors is a great way to awaken the palate. The two bitter ingredients here—Treviso radicchio and pomegranate—cancel each other out for a refreshing way to start a meal. This is the perfect example of how two negatives make a positive!

TREVISO, POMEGRANATE & PISTACHIOS

½ cup (2 oz/60 g) pistachio nuts

1 tbsp pure olive oil

Kosher salt and freshly ground black pepper

4 heads Treviso radicchio

1 pomegranate

3 tbsp Pomegranate & Chile Vinaigrette (page 161)

Wedge of pecorino cheese for shaving

Preheat the oven to 350°F (180°C). In a small bowl, toss the pistachios with the olive oil and season lightly with salt and pepper. Spread the pistachios on a small rimmed baking sheet and toast in the oven until dry and fragrant, about 5 minutes. Transfer to a plate to cool.

Using a large knife, split each head of radicchio in half lengthwise. Remove the core from each radicchio half with a V-shaped cut. Cut 4 of the halves in half again lengthwise. Cut the remaining 4 halves crosswise into ribbons 1 inch (2.5 cm) wide. Put all of the radicchio in a large bowl.

Remove the seeds from the pomegranate: Cut the pomegranate in half crosswise. Working over a deep bowl filled halfway with water, place the fruit half in your hand with the exposed seeds facing down and your fingers slightly apart. Using a wooden spoon, rap firmly on the pomegranate to release the seeds into the water. Repeat with the other half. You should have about ½ cup (3 oz/90 g) seeds.

Add the pomegranate seeds and toasted pistachios to the radicchio and season with salt and pepper. Drizzle the vinaigrette over the top and mix gently to coat evenly. Using a vegetable peeler, shave a few pecorino curls over the top and serve right away.

SERVES 4

Every Christmas Eve when I was growing up in New England, our family sat down to the Feast of the Seven Fishes, which is an Italian holiday tradition. Now, each year at Incanto, I include this dish from my childhood on the menu the week before Christmas.

BACCALÀ, BROCCOLI RABE & LEMONS

½ lb (250 g) salt cod fillet

½ white onion

2 cloves garlic

1 bunch fresh thyme

1 bay leaf

1 tbsp extra-virgin olive oil, plus more for brushing

1 cup (4 oz/125 g) coarse dried bread crumbs

2 tbsp chopped fresh flat-leaf parsley

1 tsp chopped fresh thyme

1 tsp finely grated lemon zest

Kosher salt and freshly ground black pepper

1 bunch broccoli rabe, tough stem ends trimmed

1 lemon, preferably Meyer, cut into slices ¼ inch (6 mm) thick

¼ tsp chile flakes

3 tbsp Meyer Lemon Vinaigrette (page 160)

In a large bowl, cover the salt cod with water and refrigerate for 24 hours, changing the water 2 or 3 times. Drain the cod, transfer to a saucepan, and add 8 cups (64 fl oz/2 l) water, the onion, garlic, thyme, and bay. Bring slowly to a simmer over medium heat. Simmer until the cod flakes easily with a fork, about 20 minutes. Transfer the cod to a plate to cool.

In a sauté pan over medium heat, warm the 1 tablespoon olive oil. Add the bread crumbs and stir until golden, about 4 minutes. Add the parsley, chopped thyme, and lemon zest and stir for 1 minute. Season with salt and pepper and spread in a shallow pan to cool completely. Plunge the broccoli rabe into a pan of boiling salted water until bright green, about 3 minutes. Drain and immerse in ice water to cool completely. Drain again, pat dry, and set aside.

Preheat a stove-top grill pan over high heat. Brush the lemon slices with olive oil and season with salt. Grill, turning once, until charred on both sides, 2–4 minutes total.

Flake the cooled cod into a bowl, discarding any bones and skin. Season with pepper, the chile flakes, and 1 tablespoon of the vinaigrette and toss gently to coat. In another bowl, season the broccoli rabe with salt and pepper, toss with the remaining 2 tablespoons vinaigrette, and transfer to a platter. Top with the salt cod, 2–3 tablespoons of the bread crumbs, and the lemon slices. (Reserve the remaining bread crumb mixture for another use.) Serve right away.

SERVES 4-6

When roasting, chestnuts have a very distinct smell that remind me of vendors on street corners and roadsides on the East Coast and in Europe. Juniper enhances the nuttiness of the dish and buckwheat honey adds a note of bitterness to round out the sweetness of the pears.

PEARS, ROASTED CHESTNUTS & BITTER HONEY

8 chestnuts

1 tsp juniper-infused balsamic vinegar (see Sources)

1 tbsp fresh lemon juice

1 tbsp extra-virgin olive oil

1 Anjou pear

1 red Bosc pear

Pinch of juniper berries, crushed in a mortar and then finely minced

Kosher salt

4 tbsp (2 oz/60 g) rendered duck fat

Buckwheat honey for drizzling (see Sources)

Preheat the oven to 500°F (260°C). Using a chestnut knife or a small, sharp knife, score the domed top of each chestnut with an X and place in a small roasting pan. Roast the chestnuts until the skins blister and begin to peel back from the scored marks, 10–15 minutes. Remove the chestnuts from the oven and let them cool just until they can be handled. Then, using your fingers, peel the nuts, removing both the hard outer shell and the beige, thin skin right below it. Break each chestnut into small pieces.

In a large bowl, whisk together the vinegar, lemon juice, and olive oil. Quarter each pear lengthwise, cut away the core, and then cut each quarter lengthwise into thin wedges. Add the wedges to the lemon juice mixture. Measure ¼ teaspoon of the minced juniper berries, add to the bowl, season with salt, and toss to mix well. (Reserve or discard any remaining juniper.) Set aside.

Line a plate with paper towels. In a sauté pan over medium-high heat, warm the duck fat until melted. Add the chestnut pieces and sauté until golden brown, about 4 minutes. Transfer the chestnuts to the towel-lined plate to drain. Season with salt and keep warm.

Arrange the pears on a platter or divide between individual plates. Arrange the chestnuts on the platter or plates around the pears. Dip a spoon in the buckwheat honey, pull it out, and let the honey flow off of the spoon back into the container. When only a thin stream is falling from the tip of the spoon, move the spoon over the salad and drizzle the honey over the top in a circular pattern. Serve right away.

SERVES 2

In winter, my mother often roasted acorn squash for supper and I couldn't get enough of it. I created this dressed-up version of that old family favorite in her honor, adding creamy stracciatella cheese.

ACORN SQUASH, STRACCIATELLA & SAGE

1 acorn squash

Kosher salt and freshly ground black pepper

1 bunch fresh sage

4 tbsp (2 oz/60 g) unsalted butter

2 bay leaves

2 tbsp sherry vinegar

¼ lb (125 g) stracciatella or burrata cheese

Preheat the oven to 350°F (180°C).

Cut the squash in half lengthwise and scoop out the seeds. Season the cut sides of the squash with salt and pepper. Pick the leaves from the sage sprigs and reserve. In a roasting pan just large enough to accommodate the squash halves, combine the sage stems, 1 cup (8 fl oz/250 ml) water, 2 tablespoons of the butter, and the bay, spreading the herbs evenly over the bottom of the pan. Place the squash halves, skin side down, in the pan.

Roast the squash until tender when pierced with a knife, about 1¼ hours. Transfer the squash halves to a cutting board and cut each half in half lengthwise.

In a sauté pan over high heat, melt the remaining 2 tablespoons butter. Add the squash pieces, cut side down, and sear until nicely browned, basting the whole time with the butter. Turn and sear the second cut sides until browned, continuing to baste. Add the sage leaves and then pour in the vinegar and deglaze the pan, stirring to dislodge any browned bits from the pan bottom.

Transfer the squash pieces to a warmed platter. Top each piece with one-fourth of the cheese and then drench with the butter and sage leaves. Serve right away.

SERVES 4

This is a very simple dish, so be sure that each ingredient is properly cooked. Potatoes, truffles and egg; what more do you need? This is a great rustic-but-elegant dish to serve on New Year's Eve.

POACHED EGG, ROSE FINN POTATOES & TRUFFLES

10 small Rose Finn potatoes

1–2 tsp seasoned rice or distilled white vinegar

2 large eggs

1 tbsp unsalted butter

Kosher salt and freshly cracked black pepper

2 tbsp minced fresh chives

1 fresh black truffle

In a saucepan, combine the potatoes with salted water to cover, bring to a boil over high heat, reduce the heat to a simmer, and cook until just tender when pierced with a knife, 15–20 minutes. Drain the potatoes and let cool.

To poach the eggs, pour water to a depth of 2 inches (5 cm) into a deep sauté pan. Add the vinegar, bring to a boil over high heat, and reduce the heat until the water is just under a boil. Break one egg into a small cup and gently slip the egg into the water. Working quickly, repeat with the remaining egg, spacing the eggs well apart. With a spoon, nudge the egg whites closer to the yolks. Remove the pan from the heat, cover the pan, and let the eggs stand until the whites are firm and the yolks are glazed but still liquid, about 4 minutes.

While the eggs are standing, in a sauté pan over medium heat, melt the butter. Add the potatoes and cook, tossing occasionally, until the potatoes are warmed through, about 5 minutes. Season with salt and pepper and toss well. Divide the potatoes between individual bowls and sprinkle evenly with the chives.

When the eggs are ready, using a slotted spoon, pick them up, one at a time, blot them briefly on paper towels, and place an egg on top of each serving of potatoes. Season the eggs lightly with salt and pepper. Using a truffle slicer or a handheld mandoline or vegetable slicer, thinly shave the truffle directly over the eggs, covering them completely. Serve right away.

SERVES 2

This is the Italian version of egg drop soup. I use a rich broth and then mix in eggs and Parmesan cheese, which form small shreds, and fresh matsutake mushrooms. If you can't find matsutake powder, you can pulverize dried porcini in a spice grinder.

CHICKEN & MATSUTAKE STRACCIATELLA SOUP

4 matsutake mushrooms

8 cups (64 fl oz/2 l) Chicken Stock (page 164)

1 fresh thyme sprig

1 bay leaf

1 large egg

2 large egg whites

1 tbsp grated Parmigiano-Reggiano cheese

½ tsp matsutake powder (see Sources)

Kosher salt and freshly ground black pepper

2 tbsp minced fresh chives

Trim the stems from the mushrooms and reserve the stems. Using a mandoline or other vegetable slicer, slice the mushroom caps paper-thin and set aside.

In a large saucepan over medium heat, combine the stock, thyme, bay, and mushroom stems, bring to a simmer, and cook for 10 minutes. Do not allow the stock to boil. Remove from the heat and let steep for 15 minutes.

Meanwhile, in a bowl, whisk together the whole egg, egg whites, Parmigiano-Reggiano, and matsutake powder until well blended. Transfer to a measuring pitcher with a spout.

When the stock has finished steeping, pour it through a fine-mesh sieve into a clean large saucepan. Place the pan over medium heat and bring the stock to a gentle simmer. Swirl the stock to create a vortex and then slowly drizzle in the egg mixture. It should form long, wispy strings. Do not allow the stock to boil or the strings will break and the soup will be ruined. When the egg strings have just set, add the sliced mushrooms and cook for 1 minute. Season to taste with salt and pepper.

To serve, ladle the hot soup into warmed individual bowls or a soup terrine and garnish with the chives. Serve right away.

SERVES 6

This is my play on Caesar salad. I use escarole instead of romaine, which is denser and more flavorful and stands up to the strong flavor of anchovy. Shaving Buddha's hand citron into the salad adds a refreshing brightness. This salad pairs well with hearty braised meats.

ESCAROLE, CITRON & ANCHOVY

ANCHOVY DRESSING

2 marinated white anchovy fillets

1 salt-packed anchovy, soaked in cold water for 5 minutes, drained, filleted, and rinsed

1 small clove garlic

Finely grated zest and juice of ½ lemon

1 tsp Champagne vinegar

½ cup (4 fl oz/125 ml) extra-virgin olive oil

Kosher salt and freshly ground black pepper

Sugar, if needed

Kosher salt and freshly ground black pepper

2 large eggs

1 head young escarole

1 Buddha's hand citron

½ cup (½ oz/15 g) fresh flat-leaf parsley leaves

6 marinated white anchovy fillets, chopped

To make the dressing, in a mortar, combine the white and salt-packed anchovies, garlic, and lemon zest and pound with a pestle until a paste forms. Transfer the paste to a bowl and whisk in the lemon juice and vinegar and then whisk in the olive oil. Season with salt and pepper. Taste and adjust the flavor balance with a little sugar if needed.

Bring a saucepan three-fourths full of water to a boil over high heat. Have ready a large bowl of salted ice water. Add the eggs to the boiling water and set a timer for 8 minutes. When the timer goes off, use a slotted spoon to transfer the eggs to the ice bath to cool. Once cool, peel and coarsely chop the eggs.

Separate the leaves from the escarole head. Use only the tender, pale inner leaves for this salad. Reserve the outer dark leaves for cooking. Cut off one-fourth of the "fingers" from the Buddha's hand, then, using a mandoline, shave them.

In a large bowl, combine the escarole leaves, the shaved Buddha's hand, and the parsley. Drizzle with the dressing and toss well.

Divide the salad evenly among individual plates. Garnish each salad with one-fourth of the chopped anchovies and the chopped egg. Using the mandoline, shave additional slices of the Buddha's hand over each salad. Grind pepper over the top and serve.

SERVES 6

The Alto Adige region of Italy is heavily influenced by Germany, and you often find dishes using cabbage there. I like to serve cabbage raw, as it has a great texture and refreshing mustard-like quality.

SAVOY CABBAGE, CHANTERELLES & RICOTTA SALATA

½ head Savoy cabbage

8 oz (250 g) chanterelle mushrooms, brushed clean

3 tbsp fresh flat-leaf parsley leaves, coarsely chopped

1 tbsp olive oil

2 shallots, sliced paper-thin

Kosher salt and freshly ground black pepper

1 tbsp whole-grain mustard

2 tbsp Champagne vinegar

3 tbsp extra-virgin olive oil

Wedge of *ricotta salata* cheese for shaving

Using a chef's knife, remove the core from the cabbage and then cut crosswise into thin shreds. Using a paring knife, very lightly scrape the mushroom stems to remove just the outer golden layer and dirt and then trim just the ends. Cut any larger mushrooms in half through the stem.

In a large bowl, combine the cabbage and parsley and toss to combine. In a saucepan over medium heat, warm the olive oil for 1 minute. Add the chanterelles and cook, tossing occasionally, until slightly tender and golden, about 4 minutes. Add the shallots and season lightly with salt (this helps extract some of the flavor from the vegetables) and continue to cook, tossing, until the shallots wilt and the mushrooms are tender, about 4 minutes longer. Pour the mushrooms and shallots into the bowl with the cabbage and toss well.

In a small sauté pan, stir together the mustard and vinegar to combine. Place over medium heat and warm, stirring constantly, for about 1 minute. Add the extra-virgin olive oil and swirl the pan until the ingredients are emulsified. Immediately pour the contents of the pan over the cabbage mixture and toss well. Season to taste with salt and pepper.

Divide the mushroom and cabbage mixture among individual plates. Using a vegetable peeler, shave some *ricotta salata* over each serving. Serve right away.

SERVES 4

Bruschetta is really just an open-faced sandwich. Once you have made all of the components—yes, that takes some time—the assembly is simple: creamy white bean puree spread on grilled bread and topped with a mix of rich duck confit, tart pickled onions, and peppery watercress.

DUCK CONSERVA & WHITE BEAN BRUSCHETTA

DUCK CONSERVA

6 duck legs

Kosher salt and freshly ground black pepper

2 tsp fennel seeds, ground

1 bunch fresh thyme

6 bay leaves

20 garlic cloves, crushed

1 lemon

4–6 cups (2–3 lb/1–1.5 kg) rendered duck fat

1 cup (7 oz/220 g) dried cannellini beans

½ carrot, peeled and halved

½ fennel bulb, trimmed and halved lengthwise

½ yellow onion

1 garlic head, split crosswise

1 bay leaf

1 fresh rosemary sprig

(continued)

To prepare the duck, working over a shallow bowl, season the duck legs on both sides with 2 tablespoons salt, 2 teaspoons pepper, and the fennel seeds. Gather up any spices that fell into the bowl and press them into the legs until they adhere. Place the duck legs in the bowl and add the thyme, bay, and garlic cloves. Using a vegetable peeler, remove the zest from the lemon in strips, letting them fall into the bowl. Distribute the herbs, garlic, and zest strips evenly among the duck legs. Cover and refrigerate overnight.

Preheat the oven to 250°F (120°C). Put the duck fat in the oven while it is heating to make the duck fat easier to work with.

Arrange the duck legs in a single layer in a baking pan. Pour in the duck fat just to cover. Place in the oven and cook until tender when tested with a small sharp knife, about 2 hours.

Remove the duck legs from the oven, let cool to room temperature, cover, and refrigerate overnight.

Pick over the beans, discarding any grit or misshapen beans. Rinse the beans under cold running water, transfer to a large pot, add water to cover by 2 inches (5 cm), and let stand overnight.

The next day, drain the soaked beans and return them to the pot. Add 1½ cups (1.5 l) water, the carrot, fennel, onion, garlic, bay, and rosemary. Place over medium heat, bring to a simmer, cover, and cook for 1 hour. Reduce the heat so the beans are barely simmering and continue to cook until the beans are just tender, (continued)

2 tbsp extra-virgin olive oil

Kosher salt and freshly
ground black pepper

Sherry vinegar

¼ tsp ground Aleppo
pepper

4 slices coarse country
bread, about 1 inch
(2.5 cm) thick

1 small bunch watercress,
tough stems removed

¼ cup (2 oz/60 g)
well-drained Pickled Red
Onions (page 167)

1–2 hours. The timing will depend on the age of the beans. Remove from the heat and let the beans cool in the cooking liquid. Remove the carrot, fennel, onion, and garlic and reserve. Remove and discard the bay and rosemary.

Drain the cooked beans, reserving the cooking liquid. Transfer the beans to a food processor and add the reserved carrot, fennel, and onion. Squeeze the garlic from the skins into the blender and discard the skins. With the motor running, slowly drizzle in the olive oil and process until smooth, about 5 minutes. If the purée is too thick, add a little of the cooking liquid. You want it to be spreadable, like hummus. Season with salt and pepper and then taste and adjust the flavor balance with vinegar, if needed. Season with the Aleppo pepper and set aside. (Do not season the purée too heavily, as you will be using the flavorful duck jus to reheat it.)

To remove the duck legs from the cold fat, preheat the oven to 300°F (150°C).

Place the pan holding the duck legs in the oven until the fat melts. Remove the duck legs from the fat and set them aside on a plate. Strain the contents of the pan through a fine-mesh sieve into a clear glass container. Let stand until the fat rises to the top and the jus sinks to the bottom, about 20 minutes. Using a ladle, transfer the fat to a sealable container. Reserve the duck jus for heating the bean purée, if needed.

Separate the duck meat from the bones and discard the bones, skin, and any cartilage. (It is easiest to do this when the meat is warm.) Using your fingers, pull the duck meat into large shreds. Place the meat in a bowl and keep warm.

Prepare a medium-hot fire in a charcoal or gas grill or preheat a stove-top grill pan over medium-high heat.

Brush both sides of each bread slice with some of the duck fat. (Cover and refrigerate the remaining duck fat for another use.) Place the bread slices on the grill and let cook undisturbed until crisp, but not burnt, and brown grill marks are starting to form. The timing will depend upon the bread you use and the heat of your grill—pick up an edge using tongs and take a peek to check for doneness. Using the tongs, rotate each slice 90 degrees and leave undisturbed for several seconds (take another peek to check) to create uniform cross-hatching on the underside. Using the tongs, turn the slices over and repeat to crosshatch the second side the same way. Be sure the bread is evenly grilled and not overcooked.

Meanwhile, transfer the bean purée to a heavy saucepan, place over low heat, and warm, stirring frequently, until hot. If the purée seems too thick, thin it with a little of the duck jus. Remove the pan from the heat.

Spread a thick layer of the bean purée on each slice of grilled bread. Cut each bread slice in half on a 30-degree angle and place the halves on a plate. Top the bread slices with the duck meat, dividing it evenly. Top with the watercress and pickled red onions and serve.

SERVES 4

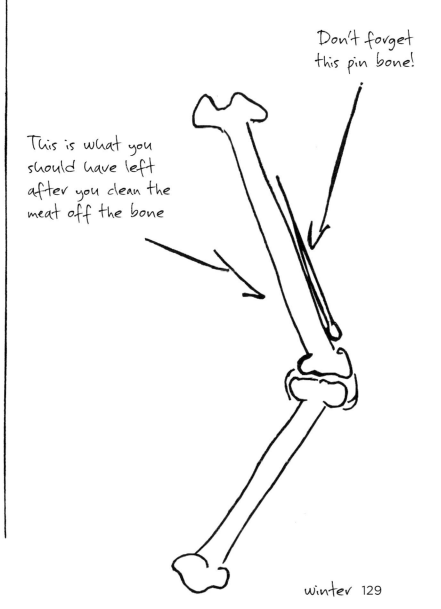

Don't forget this pin bone!

This is what you should have left after you clean the meat off the bone

This is a dish for a cold and snowy night. The beans are cooked in advance with fennel, carrot, and onion, and then simmered again with the sausages, a scattering of fresh sage leaves, and a few garlic cloves until all of the flavors are well blended.

SAUSAGES & BEANS

1 lb (500 g) dried Gigante beans

3 qt (3 l) Pork Stock (page 165)

6 cloves garlic, crushed

1 fennel bulb, trimmed and halved lengthwise

1 carrot, peeled

1 yellow onion

4 canned plum tomatoes, chopped

1 tbsp olive oil

4 sweet Italian sausages, preferably Boccalone brand (see Sources)

4 or 5 fresh sage leaves

Kosher salt and freshly ground black pepper

Pick over the beans, discarding any grit or misshapen beans. Rinse the beans under cold running water, transfer to a large pot, add water to cover by 2 inches (5 cm), and let stand overnight.

Drain the beans and return them to the pot. Add the stock, 2 of the garlic cloves, the fennel, carrot, onion, and tomatoes. Place over medium heat, bring to a simmer, cover, and cook for 1 hour. Reduce the heat so the beans are barely simmering and continue to cook until the beans are just tender, 2–3 hours. The timing will depend on the age of the beans. Remove from the heat and let the beans cool in the cooking liquid. Remove and discard the carrot, fennel, and onion.

Select a heavy frying pan large enough to hold the sausages and the beans without crowding. Add the olive oil to the pan and warm over medium heat. Add the sausages and the remaining 4 garlic cloves and cook the sausages, turning as needed, until well browned on all sides. Add the sage and heat until it sizzles. Then add the beans and their cooking liquid and cook, stirring occasionally, until heated through, about 5 minutes.

Season with salt and pepper and continue to simmer, stirring gently, until the sausages are cooked through and the bean liquid has thickened. As you stir, be careful not to break up the beans. Divide among shallow bowls and serve right away.

SERVES 4

Ham hocks are like smoky pork osso buco. They're good with just about anything you put them with, but I think the combination of the hock meat, Umbrian green lentils, and Swiss chard is perfect.

HAM HOCKS, LENTILS & CHARD

HAM HOCKS

2 ham hocks, about 1 lb (500 g) each

½ yellow onion

1 carrot, halved

1 celery rib, halved

3 bay leaves

LENTILS

½ cup (3½ oz/105 g) small green lentils, preferably Umbrian (see Sources), picked over and rinsed

1 head garlic, split crosswise

½ yellow onion

½ carrot, halved

1 bay leaf

Kosher salt and freshly ground black pepper

(continued)

To prepare the ham hocks, combine the hocks, onion, carrot, celery, bay, and 3 cups (24 fl oz/750 ml) water in a pressure cooker. Following the manufacturer's instructions, secure the lid in place, bring up to full pressure, and cook for 30 minutes. Let the pressure release naturally for 10 minutes, then uncover. Remove the hocks from the pressure cooker and set aside on a plate to cool until they can be handled. Strain the broth and discard the solids. Measure 1½ cups (12 fl oz/375 ml) of the broth and reserve for the recipe. Discard the remainder or reserve for another use. Remove the meat from the ham hocks, discarding the skin and bones. Measure 1 cup (6 oz/185 g) of the meat and reserve for the recipe. Cover and refrigerate the remaining meat for another use.

To cook the lentils, in a saucepan, combine the lentils and 3 cups (24 fl oz/750 ml) water and bring to a boil over high heat. Immediately remove the pan from the heat, drain the lentils, rinse under cold running water, and return the lentils to the pan. Add 3 cups (24 fl oz/750 ml) water, the garlic, onion, carrot, and bay to the pan, place over medium heat, and bring to a simmer. Cook just until the lentils are tender but have not split, 25–30 minutes. Drain the lentils well and discard the vegetables and bay. Spread the lentils on a rimmed baking sheet, season with salt and pepper, and let cool completely. Measure ½ cup (3 oz/90 g) of the lentils, cover, and refrigerate until needed for the recipe. Cover and refrigerate the remaining lentils for another use. (continued)

4 Swiss chard leaves, preferably with white ribs

1 tbsp extra-virgin olive oil, plus more for drizzling

¼ cup (1½ oz/45 g) finely diced yellow onion

¼ cup (1½ oz/45 g) finely diced peeled carrot

2 tbsp thinly sliced garlic

1 cup (8 fl oz/250 ml) Chicken Stock (page 164)

About 1 tsp sherry vinegar

Kosher salt and freshly ground black pepper

Separate the green leaves from the chard ribs. Separately cut the leaves and ribs crosswise into strips ½ inch (12 mm) wide. Set aside. In a heavy saucepan over medium-high heat, warm the olive oil. Add the onion, carrot, chard ribs, and garlic to the pan and cook, stirring occasionally, until the vegetables are tender, about 4 minutes. Add the reserved lentils, the ham-hock meat, the hock broth, and the chicken stock and bring to a gentle simmer. Add the chard leaves and cook until the leaves are tender, about 4 minutes.

Taste for seasoning and adjust with vinegar. Taste again and adjust the seasoning with salt and pepper, if needed. (The ham hock broth can sometimes be salty enough.)

To serve, ladle into warmed bowls and top each serving with a drizzle of olive oil. Serve right away.

SERVES 4

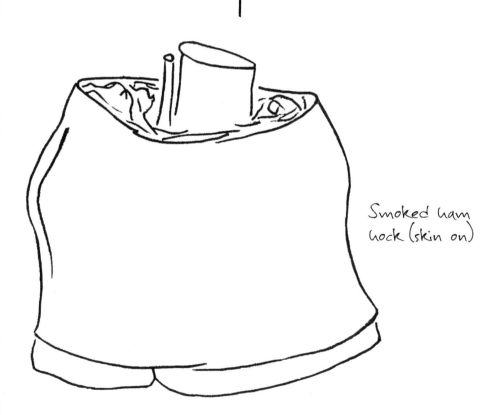

Smoked ham hock (skin on)

This is the classic antipasto that everyone loves: spreadable chicken liver on a piece of grilled bread. Finish each piece with a bit of coarse salt and you have the perfect starter for dinner—it's also a great afternoon snack. Serve with a glass of vin santo, and you are set!

TUSCAN-STYLE CHICKEN LIVERS

1½ lb (750 g) chicken livers, trimmed of any sinew or green or brown patches

3 shallots, sliced

¼ cup (2 fl oz/60 ml) *vin santo*

2 tsp fresh thyme leaves

1 fresh bay leaf

Finely grated zest of 1 orange

Kosher salt and freshly ground black pepper

Small pinch of licorice powder (see Sources)

4 tbsp (2 oz/60 g) rendered duck fat, plus more melted duck fat for sealing

3½ tbsp (1¾ oz/50 g) unsalted butter

24 baguette slices

In a shallow bowl, combine the chicken livers, shallots, *vin santo*, thyme, bay, orange zest, 2 teaspoons salt, ½ teaspoon pepper, and the licorice powder and mix well. Cover and refrigerate for 3 hours.

Remove and discard the bay leaf from the chicken livers. In a large sauté pan over high heat, warm the duck fat. When it is hot, working in batches so as not to crowd the pan, use a slotted spoon to transfer the chicken livers and shallots to the pan. Cook, turning as needed, until the livers are well colored on the outside and pink at the center, about 4 minutes. As each batch is ready, transfer it to a food processor. Pour the remaining marinade into the pan, stir up the browned bits, and add the contents of the pan to the food processor.

Process the liver mixture until smooth. With the motor running, slowly add the butter until the mixture is emulsified. Pass the mixture through a tamis (drum sieve) into a bowl. Pack the mixture into one or more ramekins and top with a thin layer of duck fat to seal. Cover and refrigerate for at least 6 hours or up to 4 days.

Just before serving, preheat a stove-top grill pan over medium-high heat. Place the baguette slices on the grill rack and grill, turning once, until etched with grill marks and crisp on both sides, about 2 minutes on each side.

To serve, set out the ramekin, the baguette slices, and a spoon.

SERVES 6

This is so perfect! What a pairing: bone marrow, also known as "God's butter," and caviar are an ideal mix of rich and buttery with salty and refreshing. The herb salad on top cuts the richness, and grilled bread nearly makes it a meal. Save this for that special night when you want to show off a bit.

"SURF & TURF" BONE MARROW, CAVIAR & HERBS

18 center-cut marrowbones, each 2 inches (5 cm) long and split lengthwise

Sea salt, preferably Halen Môn (see Sources), and freshly ground black pepper

Extra-virgin olive oil for brushing and dressing

12 slices coarse country bread

1 lemon

1/3 cup (1/3 oz/10 g) fresh chive batons (1/2-inch/12-mm lengths)

1/3 cup (1/3 oz/10 g) fresh tarragon leaves

1/3 cup (1/3 oz/10 g) fresh chervil leaves

1/3 cup (1/3 oz/10 g) fresh flat-leaf parsley leaves

1/3 cup (1/3 oz/10 g) celery leaves

Splash of fresh lemon juice

4 oz (125 g) caviar, the best you can afford

Remove the marrowbones from the refrigerator 2 hours before you plan to roast them to ensure the marrow cooks evenly. Season them with salt, pepper, and olive oil and stand them upright in a roasting pan. Preheat the oven to 500°F (260°C).

Preheat a stove-top grill pan over medium heat. Brush the bread slices on both sides with olive oil and then season on both sides with salt and pepper. Grill the bread, turning once, until etched with grill marks and crisp on both sides, about 2 minutes on each side. Alternatively, preheat the broiler and toast the prepared baguette slices on both sides. When the bread is ready, rub each slice on one side with the whole lemon, releasing the natural oils of the zest to flavor the bread.

Roast the marrowbones until the marrow is soft in the center of the bones and warm throughout, 8–10 minutes.

Just before the marrowbones are ready, in a bowl, combine the chives, tarragon, chervil, parsley, and celery leaves. Drizzle with a little olive oil and the lemon juice and toss to coat evenly.

Transfer the bones to a warmed platter, and top each bone with a spoonful of the caviar. Scatter the herb salad over the bones and place the bread on the platter. Serve right away with small spoons or spreaders.

SERVES 6

The ham puree underneath the charred brussels sprouts comes as a nice surprise when you dig to the bottom of the bowl. Keep this recipe in mind as a great way to use the end of your country ham.

CHARRED BRUSSELS SPROUTS, WALNUTS & COUNTRY HAM

COUNTRY HAM PURÉE

½ lb (250 g) boneless country ham (see Sources)

½ yellow onion

1 carrot, peeled and halved

½ fennel bulb, trimmed

4 cloves garlic

20 brussels sprouts, ends trimmed and halved lengthwise

2 tbsp rendered duck fat

¼ cup (1 oz/30 g) walnuts

2 tbsp fresh sage leaves

1 tbsp unsalted butter

Kosher salt and freshly ground black pepper

To make the country ham purée, combine the ham, onion, carrot, fennel, garlic, and 2½ cups (20 fl oz/625 ml) water in a pressure cooker. Following the manufacturer's instructions, secure the lid in place, bring up to full pressure, and cook for 15 minutes. Let the pressure release naturally for 10 minutes, then uncover and let cool slightly. Transfer the contents of the pressure cooker to a blender and process until smooth. If the purée seems too thick, add a little water. Pour into a small saucepan and set aside.

Plunge half of the brussels sprouts into a pan of boiling salted water and boil until just tender, about 3 minutes. Using a wire skimmer, transfer the sprouts to an ice-water bath to cool completely, then remove from the bath and reserve. Repeat with the remaining brussels sprouts, adding more ice to the ice-water bath if necessary. Pat the brussels sprouts dry.

In a sauté pan over high heat, warm the duck fat. When it is hot, add the brussels sprouts and sauté until golden brown on both sides, 3–5 minutes. Add the walnuts and cook, stirring occasionally, until toasted, about 2 minutes. Add the sage and butter and swirl the pan to melt the butter and crisp the sage. Season with salt and pepper.

While the brussels sprouts are cooking, warm the ham purée over medium heat until hot, being careful not to scorch it.

To serve, pour a small pool of ham purée in the bottom of each warmed bowl. Divide the brussels sprouts mixture evenly among the bowls and serve right away.

SERVES 4

Lardo is thought by some to be a bad word. Those who opt to taste it, however, discover that it is creamy, delicate, and flavorful. In this dish, the richness of the lardo is balanced by the tartness of the pear.

ASIAN PEAR, LARDO & ROSE THYME

2 Asian pears, preferably Shinku

Flaky sea salt, preferably Halen Môn, and freshly ground black pepper

¼ lb (125 g) *Iberico de bellota lardo,* preferably Boccalone brand, or country ham (see Sources), sliced thinly

¼ cup (¼ oz/7 g) fresh rose thyme leaves

¼ cup (¼ oz/7 g) pesticide-free rose geranium petals

Extra-virgin olive oil for drizzling

Cut each pear in half lengthwise and then cut each half lengthwise into quarters. Cut away the core from each wedge.

To serve, arrange 4 wedges on each plate and season with salt and pepper. Drape 5 *lardo* slices over the pear wedges on each plate. Sprinkle the plates with the rose thyme and geranium petals, dividing evenly, and then drizzle each salad with olive oil. Serve right away.

SERVES 4

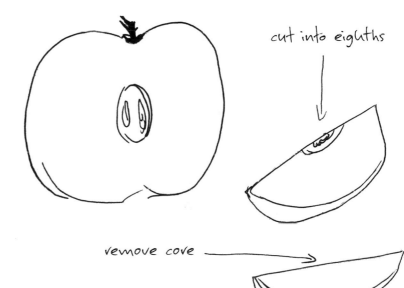

cut into eighths

remove core

The year I started at Incanto, I put this dish on the menu when our local Dungeness crab season opened. It calls for all the parts of the crab—shells, meat, guts—so none of the crab goes to waste. Not surprisingly, it is loved by my guests and dreaded by the prep cooks who have to clean and shell the crabs.

DUNGENESS CRAB, FREGOLA, CHILES & FENNEL

3½ qt (3.5 l) Court Bouillon (page 163)

2 live Dungeness crabs

4 cups (32 fl oz/1 l) Crab Stock (page 166)

Sea salt and freshly ground black pepper

1½ cups (10½ oz/330 g) *fregola*

2 tbsp extra-virgin olive oil

1 yellow onion, finely diced

1 fennel bulb, trimmed, bulb finely diced, and fronds chopped and reserved

1 clove garlic, slivered lengthwise

Chile Oil (page 161) for drizzling

In a large, tall pot, bring the court bouillon to a boil. Immerse the crabs in the liquid and boil until they turn red, about 5 minutes. Using tongs, transfer the crabs to a large plate and let cool. Working with one crab at a time, place it on its back and lift up and discard the triangular flap and intestinal vein. Turn the crab over, and snap off the hard top shell. Remove and discard the spongy gills, reserving the tommaley and the guts. Twist off the claws and legs. Using a large, heavy knife, cut the body in half from head to tail and then cut each half in half crosswise. Remove the meat from the body cavities. Using a nutcracker or mallet, crack the legs and claws and remove the meat. Transfer all the crabmeat to a bowl. Reserve the crab shells for stock.

In a large saucepan, bring the crab stock to a boil over high heat. Add a pinch of salt and the *fregola*, reduce the heat to maintain a gentle simmer, and cook, stirring occasionally, until the *fregola* is tender, 10–15 minutes. Drain, reserving the stock.

In a clean saucepan over medium-high heat, warm the olive oil. Add the onion, diced fennel, and garlic and sauté until the onion is translucent, about 5 minutes. Add the *fregola* and the reserved crab stock and bring to a boil. Remove from heat and stir in all of the crabmeat, some of the fennel fronds, and a grind of pepper. Taste and adjust the seasoning if needed.

To serve, divide among warmed individual bowls. Drizzle evenly with the chile oil, sprinkle with the remaining fennel fronds, and serve right away.

SERVES 4

The hard,
the soft

& the stinky

Here is the deal on cheese: There is no right or wrong, it all comes down to what you like, or what you are in the mood for. When I buy cheese, I ask my cheese guy, Andy, "What do you think is best right now?" Then we talk about the flavor profiles and I ask for a sample taste of the things that sound good. If I like it, I buy it. It's that simple! At Incanto, I often like to focus on one cheese and build a whole dish around it. For instance, in the spring, I like to serve a young pecorino with saba and raw fava beans. In the winter, I'll do a Blu del Moncenisio paired with hazelnuts and cardoon honey. These combinations emphasize the season and the product at its best.

When I'm cooking for a large group, I like to serve a variety of cheeses made from different milks and with different textures. Be sure to offer the right condiments that show off the individuality of each cheese. My advice to you is this: Don't be afraid go to your local cheese shop to try something new. As I say to my son, "Have a 'no thank you bite' before you decide you don't like it!" You never know what you might find.

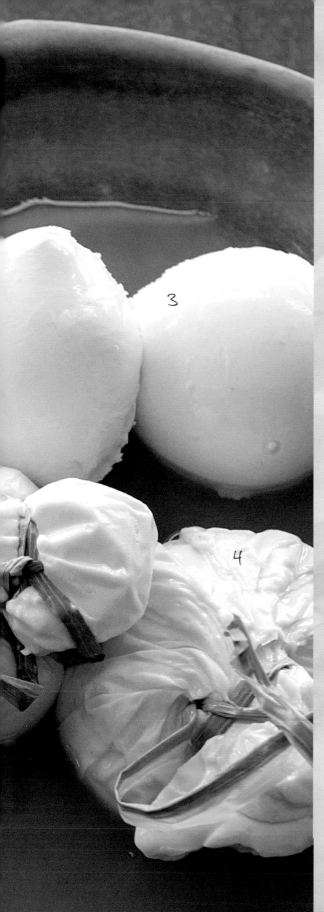

FRESH CHEESES

Fresh cheese can vary from light and delicate to very rich and creamy. Minimally aged and processed, the flavor of the raw milk comes through in this style of cheese. To retain the true flavors, fresh cheese is best served as is or barely cooked.

1. Stracciatella di Bufala

Produced from the milk of water buffalo in the Italian province of Foggia, this fresh cheese is made in the *pasta filata* style, like mozzarella, where the fresh curds are stretched and pulled to create a soft, elastic, stringy texture. I like to pair it with rich, earthy flavors, like acorn squash, sage, and brown butter (page 119).

2. Ricotta

A mild-tasting, spreadable cheese made from whey, a by-product of cheese production. Artisanal versions are moist and rich and are delicious on bruschetta with a drizzle of honey or pickled mushrooms (page 90). It also pairs well with juicy roasted figs (page 86).

3. Mozzarella di Bufala

Made from the milk of water buffalo in the Campania region, this is one of Italy's most celebrated cheeses. It has a more complex, slightly sour flavor than that of cow's milk mozzarella. Slice and serve it with fresh tomatoes, of course.

4. Burrata

This rich, creamy delicacy, once a well-kept secret in the small Italian town of Andria and now a worldwide obsession, consists of a "shell" of cow's milk mozzarella surrounding an interior of curds and cream. Burrata doesn't need a lot of embellishment: serve it topped with fruity olive oil, sea salt, and black pepper, along with toasted bread.

SOFT CHEESES

These cheeses age from the exterior inward, and remain moist inside thanks to a soft, powdery white covering known as a bloomy rind. Let the cheeses sit at room temperature for a little while before you serve them so they'll be full-flavored and ripe, and oozing with deliciousness.

1. Acquavite Brescianella

This cow's milk robiola from the Lombardy region is coated in rye seeds and soaked in grape must, then aged for 2–3 months. As it ages, it develops a fruity fullness and pleasant bite. It's a special-occasion type of cheese, so pair it with full-bodied, aged red wines or grappa.

2. Robiola Nostrana

Another cow's milk robiola produced in the Lombardy region, this cheese is never washed during the 60-day aging period. It develops a thin, edible, bloomy white rind and a mild, earthy flavor. Pair it with beer, fresh fruit, and bread.

3. Ciabra di Vacca in Foglie

Made in the small commune of Morozzo in Piedmont from pasteurized cow's milk, this sweet, milky cheese is wrapped in chestnut leaves, which protect it and impart a subtle, woodsy flavor during the 15-day aging period.

4. La Tur

From the Langhe region of Piedmont, this cylindrical cheese takes its name from the word for tower in the local dialect. A blend of cow's, goat's, and sheep's milk, it has an intensely creamy and lush texture and a sweet, buttery flavor. It's a great party cheese—serve it with bread or crackers and sparkling wine.

5. Robiola di Langa Due Latti

A blend of cow's and sheep's milk, this robiola from the Langhe region of Piedmont is lush and supple with layers of flavors ranging from fresh cream, yeasts, grasses, butter, and barnyard hay. It pairs well with fruity white wines, marmalade, and walnut or raisin bread.

1. Pecorino Romano

In Italian, *pecora* means *sheep,* so you can probably guess what kind of milk this is made from. Pecorino is made all over Italy, but the most common varieties are Romano, Toscano, Sardo, and Siciliano. Its sharp, robust flavor makes it ideal for grating over pasta dishes, risottos, and even salads (like the one with fava beans and strawberries on page 45).

2. Marzolino Rosso

This traditional, artisan version of the Tuscan Marzolino, made with sheep's milk, is a favorite of mine. The rind is treated with tomato juice, giving it a red hue. It pairs well with white wines and tangy green tomato chutney, fresh seasonal fruit, and Tuscan-style bread.

3. Testun al Barolo

A traditional intensely flavored cheese from Piedmont, testun can be made from almost any combination of milks. This one is a blend of cow's and goat's milk, coated with a thick crust of Barolo that adds a fruity tang to the robust cheese. Pair it with big, full-bodied red wines, rye bread, and something sweet, like honey or fruit chutney.

4. Ricotta Salata

When fresh ricotta cheese is salted, pressed, and dried, this tangy, dense, snow-white cheese is the result. It can be grated, shaved, crumbled, or diced for adding flavor to dishes like grilled vegetables or salads. It adds a welcome bite to my crunchy Savoy cabbage and chanterelle salad (page 125).

HARD CHEESES

The firmest-textured cheeses are made by "cooking" or heating curds until they solidify, and then pressing and aging them over a long period of time. This aging period dries and hardens the texture, and sharpens the flavor. Use them for grating over pasta or as a last-minute finish for a dish. Wrap hard cheeses in parchment and they will hold well in your refrigerator.

5. Piave Vecchio

This sharp cow's milk cheese, made in small batches in the province of Belluno in Veneto, is likened to Parmigiano-Reggiano. Some piaves are treated with preservatives, but this untreated version has a natural tan color and a nutty, caramel flavor that deepens and blossoms as the cheese ages. Shave it over a bitter-greens salad, or set it out on the table with a bowl of marinated green olives.

6. Canestrato di Moliterno

A type of pecorino made in Moliterno, a commune located right where Campania, Calabria, and Basilicata intersect. Made from goat's and sheep's milk, it has a rich, tangy flavor and a flaky texture. Shave it over fresh peas, or slice it and serve with oranges or quince chutney for an after dinner cheese course.

7. Parmigiano-Reggiano

Made from raw cow's milk and molded into large wheels, this classic Italian cheese is aged for a minimum of 1 year before being inspected to ensure quality. True Parmigiano-Reggiano has a sharp, complex, nutty taste with a strong savory flavor. Grate or shave it over pastas, pizzas, or salads, or serve a big hunk of it on a cheese plate with fruit or honey.

STINKY CHEESES

I call this the "love it or hate it" category of cheese. These cheeses have a strong, ripe, moldy scent, which gives them their distinct pungent quality. Some have veins of visible blue mold, while others have a dark yellow or orangey hue.

1. Blu Val Chiusella

A blue cheese from the Piedmontese province of Turin made from a blend of cow's and sheep's milk, and wrapped in leaves during its 60- to 90-day cellar aging. Dense, creamy, and rich with intense blue veining, it is similar to Roquefort but a bit drier. Pairs well with marmalades or *mostarda*, an Italian condiment made of candied fruit and mustard.

2. Robiola la Rustica

Produced in the Lombardy region, this cow's milk cheese has a washed, dark yellow rind with slight, natural blue-green mold in the striations on the top and sides. It is full-bodied without being overbearing. Pair it with caramelized apples or pears and hazelnuts.

3. Gorgonzola Picante

This is a cow's milk cheese from the Lombardy region that develops a powerful aroma and a sticky rind from being washed repeatedly with brine during its year or more of cave aging. Spicy and earthy, Gorgonzola *piccante* is firmer and more aggressive than its better-known sibling, Gorgonzola *dolcelatte*.

4. Bresciannella Stagionata

This smooth, sweet cheese from the Lombardy region of Italy is a close relative of taleggio. The rich flavors and lingering grassy aftertaste become more pungent as the cheese ages for between 1 and 6 months. Serve it with fruity white wine and fresh fruit, or stir some into a batch of warm polenta.

5. Blu del Moncenisio

A raw cow's milk blue produced in the Italian Alps bordering France. It's assertive, yet balanced, with notes of chocolate and cream, and a salty, savory edge. Pairs well with full-bodied, aged red wines and sweet wines, fruit chutney, rye bread, and polenta.

3

4

5

THE PERFECT CHEESE PLATTER

Building the perfect cheese platter is all about having a balance of flavors and styles of cheese.

choose different types

When choosing cheese for a platter, it's best to look for a variety of milk types, ages, and styles of cheese. Choose cheese with different flavor profiles: strong or mild, rich or salty, creamy or firm. Don't overload the platter with one style of cheese; aim to maintain a good balance. Each cheese should provide a different experience.

set out the right tools

When preparing and serving cheese, it's best to use the right tools to do the job. If you don't, you could mar the texture of the cheese or even worse, get hurt. That being said, you don't need to go out and buy a full cheese knife set; just don't use the cheese curler to try to cut the triple cream.

don't overthink it

You don't need to be an artist to arrange a cheese platter. Remember it needs to look nice, but mainly it just needs to make sense and have balance. Try to arrange the cheeses with a sense of flow, placing them in the order you want your guests to taste them. Make sure to have a variety of condiments. You want items that will complement the cheeses and help to showcase their unique flavors without overpowering them. You'll find some of my favorite condiments on page 168.

ON THE PLATTER

159

THE LARDER

LEMON VINAIGRETTE

Finely grated zest of 1 lemon

¼ cup (2 fl oz/60 ml) fresh lemon juice, plus more as needed

½ cup (4 fl oz/125 ml) pure olive oil

3 tbsp extra-virgin olive oil

Kosher salt and freshly ground black pepper

In a small bowl, whisk together the lemon zest, lemon juice, and pure olive oil until emulsified and then whisk in the extra-virgin oil. Season to taste with salt and pepper. Taste and adjust the final flavor balance with a little more lemon juice if needed. Use right away or cover and refrigerate for up to 1 day.

MAKES 1 CUP (8 FL OZ/250 ML)

MEYER LEMON VINAIGRETTE

¼ cup (2 fl oz/60 ml) fresh Meyer lemon juice

½ cup (4 fl oz/125 ml) pure olive oil

2 tbsp extra-virgin olive oil

Kosher salt and freshly ground black pepper

In a small bowl, whisk together the lemon juice and pure olive oil until emulsified and then whisk in the extra-virgin oil. Season to taste with salt and pepper. Use right away, or cover and refrigerate for up to 1 day.

MAKES ¾ CUP PLUS 2 TBSP (7 FL OZ/220 ML)

LEMON-ANCHOVY DRESSING

3 marinated white anchovy fillets

2 salt-packed anchovies, soaked in cold water for 5 minutes, drained, filleted, and rinsed

1 clove garlic

Finely grated zest and juice of 1 Meyer lemon

Juice of 1 Eureka lemon

¼ tsp Champagne vinegar

½ cup (4 fl oz/125 ml) pure olive oil

2 tbsp extra-virgin olive oil

Kosher salt and freshly ground black pepper

¼ tsp sugar, if needed

2 white anchovy fillets, chopped

In a mortar, combine the marinated anchovy fillets, the salt-packed anchovies, the garlic, and the lemon zest and pound with a pestle until a paste forms. In a bowl, whisk together both lemon juices, the vinegar, and the anchovy mixture. Whisk in the pure olive oil until emulsified and then whisk in the extra-virgin oil. Season to taste with salt and pepper. Taste and add the sugar if needed to balance any bitterness. Whisk in the chopped white anchovy, then taste again and adjust the seasoning. Use right away, or cover and refrigerate for up to 2 days.

MAKES ABOUT 1 CUP (8 FL OZ/250 ML)

BALSAMIC VINAIGRETTE

⅓ cup (3 fl oz/80 ml) balsamic vinegar, preferably O brand (see Sources)

⅓ cup (3 fl oz/80 ml) *each* pure olive oil and extra-virgin olive oil

Kosher salt and freshly ground black pepper

In a small bowl, whisk together the vinegar and pure olive oil until emulsified and then whisk in the extra-virgin oil. Season to taste with salt and pepper. Use right away, or cover and refrigerate for up to 2 days.

MAKES ABOUT 1 CUP (8 FL OZ/250 ML)

ZINFANDEL VINAIGRETTE

¼ cup (2 fl oz/60 ml) Zinfandel vinegar

Juice of 1 lemon

¼ cup (2 fl oz/60 ml) *each* pure olive oil and extra-virgin olive oil

Kosher salt and freshly ground black pepper

In a small bowl, whisk together the vinegar, lemon juice, and pure olive oil until emulsified and then whisk in the extra-virgin olive oil. Season to taste with salt and pepper. Use right away, or cover and refrigerate for up to 2 days.

MAKES ¾ CUP (6 FL OZ/180 ML)

PORT VINAIGRETTE

¼ cup (2 fl oz/60 ml) *each* Port vinegar, pure olive oil, and extra-virgin olive oil

Kosher salt and freshly ground black pepper

Splash of fresh lemon juice

In a small bowl, whisk together the vinegar and pure olive oil until emulsified and then whisk in the extra-virgin oil. Season to taste with salt and pepper and then taste and adjust the final flavor balance with the lemon juice. Use right away, or cover and refrigerate for up to 2 days.

MAKES ¾ CUP (6 FL OZ/180 ML)

POMEGRANATE & CHILE VINAIGRETTE

2 tbsp *each* Zinfandel vinegar and pomegranate molasses

1 dried cascabel chile, split and seeded

¼ cup (2 fl oz/60 ml) *each* pure olive oil and extra-virgin olive oil

¼ tsp sugar

Kosher salt and freshly ground black pepper

Splash of fresh lemon juice

In a blender, combine the Zinfandel vinegar, pomegranate molasses, and chile. With the motor running, slowly pour in both olive oils. Once the oils are incorporated, season with the sugar, ½ teaspoon salt, and pepper to

taste. Then taste and adjust the final flavor balance with the lemon juice. Use right away, or cover and refrigerate for up to 2 days.

MAKES ABOUT 1 CUP (8 FL OZ/250 ML)

CHILE OIL

2 *each* red Fresno chiles and jalapeño chiles, seeded and finely diced

¼ cup (2 fl oz/60 ml) extra-virgin olive oil

Finely grated zest and juice of 1 Meyer lemon

In a small bowl, whisk together the chiles, olive oil, and lemon zest and then whisk in the lemon juice to taste.

MAKES ABOUT ½ CUP (4 FL OZ/125 ML)

AIOLI

1 clove garlic

Kosher salt and freshly ground black pepper

1 large egg yolk

½ tsp Dijon mustard

½ cup (4 fl oz/125 ml) pure olive oil

Extra-virgin olive oil for drizzling

¼ tsp fresh lemon juice

In a mortar, combine the garlic and a pinch of salt and pound with a pestle until a paste forms. Add the egg yolk and mustard and stir with the pestle until combined. Slowly drizzle in 2 tablespoons of the pure olive oil while stirring vigorously with the pestle. Once the mixture begins to emulsify, transfer it to a bowl and slowly add the remaining pure olive oil in a slow, steady stream while whisking constantly. After the pure olive oil has been incorporated, finish by whisking in a drizzle of extra-virgin olive oil. Season to taste with salt, pepper, and the lemon juice.

To use a food processor, finely mince or mash the garlic and add it to the pure olive oil. Combine the egg yolk and mustard in the food processor and process until well blended. With the motor running, very slowly add the olive oil–garlic mixture in a fine stream until the mixture begins to emulsify. When all of the pure olive oil has been added, finish with a drizzle of extra-virgin olive oil. Season to taste with salt, pepper, and the lemon juice.

Use right away, or cover and refrigerate for up to 2 days.

MAKES ABOUT 1 CUP (8 FL OZ/250 ML)

BROVADA

1½ cups (12 fl oz/375 ml) Zinfandel vinegar, plus more as needed

¼ cup (2 fl oz/60 ml) dry red wine

3 cups (1 lb/500 g) whole grapes

1 purple turnip, peeled, cut into eighths

½ cup (4 oz/125 g) sugar, plus more as needed

Kosher salt

In a saucepan over high heat, combine the vinegar, wine, grapes, turnip, sugar, and a pinch of salt and bring to a boil. Reduce the heat to a simmer and cook until the turnip is tender, about 6 minutes. Remove from the heat and let cool slightly, then transfer to a blender, ideally a high-speed model, and process until smooth. Return the mixture to the saucepan over medium heat, bring to a simmer, and skim off any foam that forms on the surface. Taste and adjust the flavor with vinegar and sugar as needed to achieve a good balance of tart and sweet. Remove from the heat, let cool completely, transfer to a container with a tight-fitting lid, and refrigerate for 10 days before using. It will keep for up to 6 months.

MAKES ABOUT 2 CUPS (16 FL OZ/500 ML)

SALSA PICCANTE

3 red Fresno chiles

1 serrano chile

4 dried sweet peppers

2 dried cascabel chiles

¼ cup (2 fl oz/60 ml) pure olive oil

¼ red onion, finely diced

Finely grated zest and juice of 1 lemon

1 cup (1 oz/30 g) fresh flat-leaf parsley leaves, chopped

¼ cup (2 fl oz/60 ml) extra-virgin olive oil

Kosher salt and freshly ground black pepper

Stem the Fresno chiles, slit them lengthwise, and remove the seeds and ribs. Put the seeds and ribs in a blender. Finely dice the flesh and set aside. Stem the serrano chile, sweet peppers, and cascabel chiles and add them to the blender along with the pure olive oil. Blend on high speed until the oil is uniformly red, about 4 minutes. Transfer the contents of the blender to a bowl, add the diced Fresno chile flesh and the onion, and mix well. Add the lemon zest, juice, parsley, and the extra-virgin oil and whisk to combine. Season to taste with salt and pepper. Let the salsa stand for 2 hours before serving to allow the flavor to develop. Leftover salsa may be covered and refrigerated for up to 2 days.

MAKES ABOUT 1¼ CUPS (10 FL OZ/310 ML)

SALSA VERDE

½ red onion, very finely diced

Kosher salt and freshly ground black pepper

1½ tsp red wine vinegar

1 tbsp salted capers

½ cup (½ oz/15 g) *each* fresh flat-leaf parsley and chervil leaves, coarsely chopped

¼ cup (¼ oz/7 g) fresh tarragon leaves, coarsely chopped

2 tbsp minced fresh chives

1–2 cloves garlic, finely grated

½ tsp finely grated lemon zest

4–6 tbsp (2–3 fl oz/60–90 ml) extra-virgin olive oil

Splash of fresh lemon juice, if needed

Put the onion in a bowl, sprinkle with a pinch of salt, and let stand for 5 minutes. Add the vinegar and let stand for 10 minutes. In a small bowl, combine the capers with water to cover and let stand for 10 minutes.

In a bowl, combine the parsley, chervil, tarragon, chives, garlic, and lemon zest. Squeeze the vinegar from the onion and add the onion to the bowl. Drain the capers, pat dry, coarsely chop, and add to the bowl. Sprinkle with a little salt and pepper, then whisk in the olive oil to achieve the consistency you prefer. Taste and adjust the seasonings with salt and pepper and lemon juice. Let the salsa stand for 1 hour before serving to allow the flavors to develop. Leftover salsa may be covered and refrigerated for up to 2 days.

MAKES ABOUT ⅔ CUP (5 FL OZ/ 160 ML)

ANCHOVY BUTTER

1 cup (½ lb/250 g) unsalted butter, at room temperature

½ small yellow onion, finely diced

1 salt-packed anchovy, soaked in cold water for 5 minutes, drained, filleted, and rinsed

1 tbsp finely chopped marinated white anchovy fillets

2 tbsp finely chopped fresh mint leaves

Finely grated zest of ½ lemon

Kosher salt and freshly ground black pepper

In a stand mixer fitted with the paddle attachment, combine the butter, onion,

salt-packed anchovy, white anchovies, mint, and lemon zest and beat on medium speed until well combined. Season to taste with salt and pepper, mixing well. Divide the flavored butter into portions, place between 2 sheets of parchment paper, and roll each portion into a cylinder. Wrap the cylinders separately in plastic wrap and refrigerate for up to 6 days or freeze for up to 1 month.

MAKES ABOUT 1½ CUPS (12 OZ/375 G)

GARLIC CHIPS

Pure olive oil for deep-frying

10 cloves garlic

Kosher salt and freshly ground black pepper

Pour the oil to a depth of 2 inches (5 cm) into a small, heavy saucepan and heat to 350°F (180°C). While the oil is heating, using a mandoline or other vegetable slicer, carefully slice the garlic cloves lengthwise paper-thin.

When the oil is ready, working in batches, add the garlic slices to the hot oil and fry, stirring as needed to fry evenly, until golden brown, about 1 minute. Using a slotted spoon, transfer the chips to a paper towel to drain. Season lightly with salt and pepper. The chips can be made up to 3 days ahead. Transfer to an airtight container lined with clean paper towels and store at room temperature.

MAKES 8 SERVINGS

COURT BOUILLON

1⅓ cups (11 fl oz/340 ml) dry white wine

½ bunch fresh thyme

Stems from ½ bunch fresh flat-leaf parsley

1 fennel bulb, halved

1 yellow onion, halved

½ bunch celery, coarsely chopped

1 bay leaf

1½ tsp *each* black peppercorns, coriander seeds, and fennel seeds

Kosher salt

In a stockpot, combine 4 qt (4l) water, the wine, thyme, parsley, fennel, onion, celery, bay, peppercorns, coriander seeds, fennel seeds, and 1½ teaspoons salt and bring to a boil over high heat. Reduce the heat to a simmer and cook for 15 minutes to develop the flavors.

Remove the pan from the heat and strain the liquid through a fine-mesh sieve into a bowl or other vessel. Use right away, or let cool, cover, and refrigerate for up to 10 days.

MAKES ABOUT 3½ QUARTS (3.5 L)

PORCINI BRODO

2 tbsp olive oil

1 white onion, chopped

1 carrot, chopped

1 fennel bulb, trimmed and chopped

½ cup (½ oz/15 g) dried porcini mushrooms

1 bay leaf

2 fresh thyme sprigs

1 head garlic, crosswise

½ cup (4 fl oz/125 ml) dry white wine

4 cups (32 fl oz/1 l) *each* Chicken Stock (right) and Pork Stock (page 165)

Kosher salt and freshly ground black pepper

Juice of 1 lemon

In a stockpot over medium heat, warm the olive oil. Add the onion, carrot, and fennel and cook, stirring occasionally, until beginning to soften, about 5 minutes. Stir in the mushrooms, bay, thyme, and garlic and then pour in the wine and deglaze the pan, stirring to scrape

up the browned bits from the pan bottom. Cook until the wine has evaporated, about 5 minutes. Pour in both stocks, bring to a simmer, and cook very slowly for 30 minutes. The liquid should not reduce much at all, just deepen in flavor. Remove the broth from the heat and let stand for 15 minutes to infuse the flavors. Pour the broth through a cheesecloth-lined fine-mesh sieve into a large bowl. Season to taste with salt, pepper, and lemon juice. Use right away, or cover and refrigerate for up to 3 days.

MAKES 8 CUPS (64 FL OZ/2 L)

CHICKEN STOCK

4 lb (2 kg) chicken carcasses, including necks and backs

1 large yellow onion, peeled and quartered

4 carrots, peeled and halved crosswise

4 ribs celery, halved crosswise

1 leek, halved lengthwise

10 fresh thyme sprigs

10 fresh parsley stems

2 bay leaves

1 tsp *each* peppercorns, fennel seeds, and coriander seeds

2 garlic cloves, peeled

Place the chicken and the remaining ingredients in a 12-quart stockpot and add 8 quarts (8 l) cold water. Be sure the ingredients are covered by the water. Set the pot over high heat until the liquid begins to boil. Reduce the heat to medium-low so that the liquid maintains low, gentle simmer. Simmer, uncovered, for 6–8 hours. As the stock simmers, using a large metal spoon, skim the scum that forms on the surface of the stock every 15 minutes for the first hour of cooking and twice each hour for the next 2 hours of cooking. Add water as needed to keep the bones and vegetables submerged.

Carefully strain the stock through a fine-mesh sieve into another large stockpot or heatproof container, discarding the solids. Cool the stock right away in large cooler filled with ice or a sinkful of ice water until it is very cold, then cover and refrigerate overnight.

The next day, using a large spoon, scrape the solidified fat from surface of the stock. Store in a lidded container in the refrigerator for 2–3 days or in the freezer for up to 3 months.

MAKES ABOUT 4 QUARTS (4 L)

PORK STOCK

7 lb (3.5 kg) pork bones
in 2-inch (5-cm) pieces

1 pig's foot, split

2 yellow onions, chopped

1 large carrot, chopped

4 ribs celery, chopped

1 fennel bulb, chopped

2 cups (16 fl oz/500 ml)
dry white wine

1 bunch fresh thyme

1 bay leaf

1 head garlic, split crosswise

1 tbsp *each* black peppercorns,
fennel seeds, and coriander seeds

Kosher salt

Preheat the oven to 450°F (230°C).

Place the pork bones and pig's foot in a shallow roasting pan in a single layer. Roast the bones until deeply browned, about 1 hour. Remove the bones from the oven and scatter the onions, carrot, celery, and fennel over the top. Return the pan to the oven and roast until the vegetables are softened, 30 minutes.

Spoon or pour off any excess fat from the pan. Place the roasting pan on the stove top over high heat. Pour in the wine and, using a

wooden spoon, scrape up the browned bits on the pan bottom. Transfer the contents of the pan to a large stockpot. Add the thyme, bay, garlic, peppercorns, fennel seeds, coriander seeds, and 8 quarts (8 l) cold water. Bring the liquid to a boil, then reduce the heat to medium-low. Season the liquid lightly with salt. Simmer the stock until full flavored, about 4 hours, adding water as necessary to keep the vegetables and bones submerged.

Carefully strain the stock through a fine-mesh sieve into another large stockpot or heatproof container, discarding the solids. Cool the stock right away in large cooler filled with ice or a sinkful of ice water until it is very cold, then cover and refrigerate overnight.

The next day, using a large spoon, scrape the solidified fat from surface of the stock. Store in a lidded container in the refrigerator for 2–3 days or in the freezer for up to 3 months.

MAKES ABOUT 4 QUARTS (4 L)

FISH STOCK

4 lb (2 kg) white fish bones
with heads (gills removed)

Kosher salt

1 rib celery, chopped

1 fennel bulb, chopped

1 leek, washed well and chopped

1 yellow onion, peeled and chopped

1 tsp *each* whole peppercorns,
fennel seeds, and coriander seeds

½ bunch parsley stems

1 bay leaf

1 bunch fresh thyme

1 cup (8 fl oz/250 ml)
dry white wine

1 piece kombu (4-inch/10-cm
square piece)

Lay the fish bones on a rimmed baking sheet in a single layer and sprinkle lightly with salt. Let stand for 5 minutes. Rinse the salted bones under running cold water.

In a heavy stockpot, add the celery, fennel, leek, onion, peppercorns, fennel and coriander seeds, parsley stems, bay, and thyme. Place the fish bones on top, and then add 4 quarts (4 l) water and the wine. Set the pot over medium-low heat and bring the liquid just to a simmer. Let the stock simmer, undisturbed, for 45 minutes. Do not let the stock boil, or it will become cloudy. After 45 minutes, turn off the heat and let the stock stand for 15 minutes to develop the flavors.

Carefully strain the stock through a fine-mesh sieve into a heatproof container, then discard the solids. Add the kombu to the stock and let stand until completely cool. Remove the kombu. Store in a lidded container in the refrigerator for 3 days or in the freezer for up to 2 months.

MAKES ABOUT 4 QUARTS (4 L)

CRAB STOCK

1 tbsp pure olive oil

2 lb (1 kg) cracked or chopped crab shells and/or crab bodies

Crab tomalley

1 yellow onion, thinly sliced

2 ribs celery, thinly sliced

1 fennel bulb, thinly sliced

1½ cups (9 oz/280 g) chopped fresh or canned tomatoes

2 cloves garlic, crushed

¼ cup (2 fl oz/60 ml) dry white wine

2 qt (2 l) Fish Stock (left)

2 fresh bay leaves

1 tsp *each* coriander seeds and fennel seeds

2 tsp black peppercorns

4 fresh thyme sprigs

4 fresh parsley stems

Kosher salt

In a 6- to 8-qt (6- to 8-l) stockpot, warm the olive oil over medium-high heat. Add the crab shells, bodies, and tomalley and sauté the shells until they smell aromatic, about 5 minutes. Add the onion, celery, fennel, tomatoes, and garlic and continue to cook until the vegetables are tender, about 10 minutes. Pour in the wine, stirring to scrape up the browned bits on the pan bottom, and cook until the liquid is reduced by three-fourths. Add the fish stock to the pot along with the bay, coriander and fennel seeds, peppercorns, thyme, and parsley, and bring to a simmer. Simmer for 35 minutes, adding water if necessary to keep the ingredients submerged.

Season the stock lightly with salt. Taste for a rich flavor; if the flavor seems weak, simmer it for about 20 minutes longer.

Carefully strain the stock through a fine-mesh sieve into a heatproof container, discarding the solids. If you are not using the stock within 1 hour, cool the stock immediately in a sinkful of ice water until it is very cold, then cover and refrigerate overnight. Store in a lidded container in the refrigerator for up to 3 days, or freeze for up to 2 months.

MAKES ABOUT 4 QUARTS (4 L)

HERB-ROASTED GARLIC

4 heads garlic

6 fresh thyme sprigs

2 bay leaves

6 tbsp (3 fl oz/90 ml) olive oil

Kosher salt

½ tsp ground Aleppo pepper

¼ tsp sugar

Preheat the oven to 325°F (180°C).

Cut the tops off the garlic heads to expose the individual cloves. Line the bottom of a nonreactive pan with the thyme sprigs and bay leaves. Place the garlic on top of the herbs with the open tops facing up. Spoon the olive oil over the garlic cloves, being sure to coat each clove well, then sprinkle with ½ teaspoon salt, the Aleppo pepper, and sugar. Wrap the pan with aluminum foil and roast until the garlic is golden brown and tender, about 90 minutes. Be sure to check for doneness every 15 minutes during the cooking process; each head of garlic cooks differently.

SERVES 4

PICKLED CARROTS

2 bunches baby carrots

2 cups (16 fl oz/500 ml) Champagne vinegar

1 cup (8 oz/250 g) sugar

1 jalapeño chile, cut in half lengthwise

2 bay leaves

1 tsp *each* mustard seeds and whole black peppercorns

Kosher salt

Peel the baby carrots and place them in a nonreactive, heatproof container. In a saucepan over high heat, combine the vinegar, sugar, jalapeño, bay, mustard seeds, peppercorns, and ¼ teaspoon salt. Bring the liquid to a boil, and then pour over the carrots. Seal the container and let the carrots cool in the refrigerator overnight. The carrots will keep for up to 1 month in the refrigerator.

SERVES 4-6

PICKLED RED ONIONS

2 red onions

1 tsp Kosher salt

1 cup (8 fl oz/250 ml) Champagne vinegar

1 cup (8 oz/250 g) sugar

1 tsp *each* coriander seeds and fennel seeds

1 bay leaf

1 tsp yellow mustard seeds

Using a mandoline or other vegetable slicer, cut the onions into julienne. Place in a bowl, sprinkle with the salt, toss to mix, and let stand until wilted, about 10 minutes.

In a saucepan, combine the vinegar, sugar, coriander seeds, fennel seeds, and bay and bring to a boil over high heat, stirring to dissolve the sugar. Remove from the heat and let cool to room temperature. Rinse the onions, drain well, place in a bowl, and add the mustard seeds. Pour the cooled vinegar mixture through a fine-mesh sieve over the onions, submerging them in the liquid. Cover and refrigerate overnight before using. They will keep for up to 1 week.

MAKES 2 CUPS (12 OZ/370 G)

BALSAMIC CIPOLLINI ONIONS

1 tbsp pure olive oil

10 cipollini onions, peeled

2 cloves garlic

½ bunch fresh thyme

2 bay leaves

1 cup (8 fl oz/250 ml) balsamic vinegar

In a sauté pan over medium heat, warm the olive oil. Add the onions and garlic and cook until golden brown, about 4 minutes total. Add the thyme, bay, and vinegar, and stir to scrape up the browned bits on the pan bottom. Simmer the onions until tender, about 5 minutes;

take care not to over-reduce the vinegar, or it will be too sticky. Remove from the heat and cool before serving. Store in a covered container in the refrigerator for up to 2 days. Remove the garlic before serving.

SERVES 5

FIG JAM

1½ lb (750 g) Mission figs, washed

1 cup (8 oz/250 g) sugar

Juice and finely grated zest of 1 lemon

1 fresh bay leaf

Kosher salt

1 fresh fig leaf

Remove the stems from the figs and then cut the figs into quarters. In a large, heavy-bottomed saucepan, combine the figs, sugar, and lemon zest and juice. Bring to a simmer over medium-low heat, stirring constantly. Reduce the heat to low, add the bay and 1 teaspoon salt and simmer, covered, for 1 hour, stirring occasionally. Uncover the pan and continue to simmer, stirring frequently, until the mixture thickens to a jam-like consistency, 40–60 minutes. When the mixture gets quite thick, begin to stir constantly to keep it from scorching. To test for a good consistency, put a small amount of the simmering jam on a very cold saucer (put it in the freezer for a few minutes first). Put the saucer back in the freezer for 1 minute. The surface of the fruit mixture should wrinkle slightly when pushed with a finger.

Remove the jam from the heat and transfer it to a nonreactive heatproof container. Discard the bay leaf. Lay the fig leaf on the top of the warm jam, which will impart a great flavor and prevent a film from forming on the jam as it cools. Store the cooled jam in a lidded container in the refrigerator for up to 2 weeks.

MAKES 1¼ TO 1½ CUPS (10–12 FL OZ/310–375 ML)

ROSALIE'S PEPPER KNOTS

3½ cups (18 oz/560 g) all-purpose flour

1 tsp baking powder

½ tsp salt

¼ cup (2 oz/60 g) whole black peppercorns, ground

⅓ cup (.75 oz/20 g) aniseed, ground

⅓ cup (.75 oz/20 g) whole fennel seeds

1 cup (8 fl oz/250 ml) olive oil, plus more for brushing

1 cup (8 fl oz/250 ml) water

In a the bowl of a stand mixer, stir together the flour, baking powder, salt, pepper, aniseed, and fennel seeds. In another bowl, mix together the oil and water. Add the wet ingredients to the dry ingredients and, using the dough hook attachment on medium speed, mix until the dough comes together, about 5 minutes. The dough will be wet. Let the dough stand, covered, for about 15 minutes before shaping.

Preheat the oven to 350°F (180°C).

To form the knots, tear off a chunk of the dough and then, using your hands, roll it back and forth across a work surface until it becomes a log the length and thickness of a pencil. Divide the log in half crosswise, then twist each half into a circle knot. Lay the knots on an ungreased baking sheet and repeat with the remaining dough.

Brush the knots with olive oil and bake until light golden brown, 10–12 minutes. Serve warm, or cool on a wire rack and store in an airtight container for up to 2 days before serving. You can also store the unbaked dough in the freezer for up to 10 days and thaw it in the refrigerator the night before you plan to bake.

MAKES 1½ TO 2 DOZEN, DEPENDING ON HOW BIG YOUR KNOTS ARE

SOURCES

Beekind

Buckwheat Honey

1 Ferry Building # 21B
San Francisco, CA 94111

(415) 307-8682

www.beekind.com

Benton's Smoky Mountain Country Hams

Country ham

2603 Hwy 411 North
Madisonville, TN 37354

(423) 442-5003

bentonscountryhams2.com

Boccalone

Cured meats, including nduja, lardo, sanguinaccio (blood sausage), and more

1 Ferry Building #21
San Francisco, CA 94111

(415) 433-6500

www.boccalone.com

Broken Arrow Ranch

The best wild game available, such as quail, wild boar, and much more

www.brokenarrowranch.com

Casa de Case

Dried beans, bottarga, grains, juniper balsamic, olives, olive oils

224 Carl Street
San Francisco, CA 94117

(415) 759-6360

www.casadecase.com

D'artagnan

Duck fat, foie gras, quail, squab, truffles

www.dartagnan.com

Far West Fungi

Wild mushrooms such as matsutake and porcini, matsutake powder

1 Ferry Building #34
San Francisco, CA 94111-4229

www.farwestfungi.com

Ferry Plaza Farmers Market

A must-stop for anyone looking to get the best produce in the Bay Area

Ferry Building, San Francisco

Tuesdays, Thursdays & Saturdays

Fresca Italia

Italian cheeses

200 Valley Dr #14
Brisbane, CA 94005

(415) 468-9800

www.frescaitalia.com

Heritage Foods, USA

Beef, lamb, and pork

www.heritagefoodsusa.com

La Tienda

Baccalà, cured jamon, pimenton, white anchovies

www.tienda.com

Le Sanctuaire

Halen Môn salt, licorice powder, spices, pimentón, and speciality equipment

www.le-sanctuaire.com

Liberty Ducks

The best ducks around

www.libertyducks.com

Mama Lil's Peppers

These are the best pickled peppers there are (sometimes you need to just leave it to the professionals)

832 14th Avenue
Seattle, WA 98122

(206) 322-8824

www.mamalils.com

Mikune Harvest

Caviar, dried and fresh mushrooms

www.mikunewildharvest.com

Monterey Bay Aquarium Seafood Watch

The place to go to be sure you are buying what's best for our oceans

montereybayaquarium.org

Mozo

My go-to kitchen shoes

www.mozoshoes.com

Prather Ranch Meat Company

This is the place to get the best meats in San Francisco. I swear by them.

1 Ferry Building #32
San Francisco, CA 94111

415-391-0420

prmeatco.com

Shun

The best knives ever

www.kershawknives.com

Williams-Sonoma

All the best kitchen tools and equipment, including cataplanas and Vitamix blenders

www.williams-sonoma.com

INDEX

ACKNOWLEDGMENTS

Tatiana Graf, an amazing wife, mother, and business partner, the most supportive person on the planet. Thanks for always being there!

Mark Pastore, thanks for believing in me, you are a great business partner and a great friend.

The entire teams of Incanto and Boccalone, thanks for your loyalty and dedication, both past and present (except the ones whom I fired—you know who you are).

Manfred Wrembel, my right hand, for years of true loyalty and dedication.

Hector Burgos, who has been with me since day one.

Stephen Pocock, you have become the Boccalone meat master.

Michael Harlan Turkell, you stuck with me for years. Thanks for taking the best photos ever and being an amazing friend.

Simone D'Armini, for the awesome illustrations.

My mother, Susan Easton, who taught me to swear and to never stop fighting.

My son, Easton, for teaching me patience and keeping life fun.

Ravi Kapur, my brother from another mother.

Staffan Terje, the Swedish hammer, you are always so calm.

Jeremy Emmerson, you're always there when I need a hand.

Derek Dammann, the Canadian Ginger, I am always afraid to open your emails.

San Francisco, thanks for being a great city to cook and live in.

Harold McGee, for being a great friend and always taking the time answer a question. You have saved my ass so many times!

All my farmers and ranchers, thanks for bringing me the best products start with. Especially: Doug of Prather Ranch Meat Company; Cliff Hamada & family of Hamada Farms; Andy & Julia of Mariquita Farms; Don Watson of Napa Valley Lamb; Yerena Farms; Jim Reichart of Liberty Ducks; Mark Keller of Keller Crafted Meats; and all the farmers at the Ferry Plaza Farmers Market in San Francisco.

Andrew Chason, for always watching my back.

All the chefs who helped shape me with words of wisdom or just constant verbal abuse: Thank you, I probably deserved every bit of it. Especially, Mark Miller, Bob Kinkead, Traci Des Jardins, Michael Mina, and countless others.

All the chefs who came before me, thank you for paving the way with techniques and inspirations. We are always cooking from history.

The Weldon Owen team: Kara Church, Kim Laidlaw, Jennifer Newens & Hannah Rahill. Thanks for being great collaborators.

All of our diners over the years who have become not only great guests, but great friends. Thanks for spending your time with us.

If you don't see your name here, don't whine! There are just too many of you and not enough room.

And everyone who said I couldn't do it: Guess what? I did!!

MY LAST SUPPER

The dish I want to eat before I am put into the ground consists of blood sausage, oysters, a duck egg, crusty bread, and an unctuous pork stock that brings everything together. It is the ideal last supper, with air, land, and sea all in one unforgettable dish. It is rich, flavorful, and completely satisfying—in every way perfect for my last meal.

This dish is a culmination of years of eating. I barely ate anything when I was a kid. For example, I would eat raw carrots, but I wouldn't touch cooked carrots. I never ate tomatoes until I was around 21 years old! But you'd probably never guess that I was a picky eater knowing what I do today. Over the years I've traveled, worked in different restaurants, and really learned to appreciate more and more things every day. This dish is growth from near ignorance to enlightenment in what I've chosen to do with my food choices, with my career, and with who I am today. It's really honest, and there's something humbling about a dish as simple as a blood sausage, an egg, and an oyster—it's no bullshit. For me, this dish has multiple

meanings: There's
blood, which is life;
there's an egg, which is
also life; and there's an
oyster, which is an all-
encompassing ONE.
The flavors build on
one another: The
minerality from the
blood mimics the
minerality of the oyster.
The richness of the pork
stock plays off the richness
of the egg yolk. And then there's
the little herb salad, and that charred
bread to give the dish clarity. When I
combine all these things together, it's an all-encompassing
experience and I'm getting a bit of every world in one,
at the same time.

To make Chef's Last Supper, preheat the oven to 350°F (180°C). Starting in a cold ovenproof sauté pan, sear a blood sausage, preferably Boccalone sanguinaccio, on one side in butter. Flip the sausage and transfer the pan to the oven to heat the sausage through, 5-8 minutes. Meanwhile, preheat a stove-top grill pan over medium heat. Brush a slice of thick, coarse country bread on both sides with olive oil and grill until etched with grill marks and crisp on both sides. At the same time, fry a duck egg in butter in a sauté pan over medium heat until the whites are set but the yolks are still runny, about 3 minutes. Transfer the

egg to a shallow bowl and place the sausage alongside. Return the pan that you cooked the sausage in to high heat, pour in 1 cup Pork Stock (page 165), deglaze, and reduce by one-fourth. Add a pat of butter and 3 or 4 large oysters (I like Quilcene) and simmer just until the edges curl, about 1 minute. Transfer the oysters and pork stock to the bowl, sprinkle with chopped fresh chives, and serve right away. Now I can be put into the ground.